BECOMING A REAL MUSICIAN

BECOMING A REAL MUSICIAN

Inspiration and Guidance for Teachers and Parents of Musical Kids

Robert H. Woody

ROWMAN & LITTLEFIELD
Lanham • Boulder • New York • London

Published by Rowman & Littlefield
An imprint of The Rowman & Littlefield Publishing Group, Inc.
4501 Forbes Boulevard, Suite 200, Lanham, Maryland 20706
www.rowman.com

6 Tinworth Street, London SE11 5AL

Copyright © 2019 by The Rowman & Littlefield Publishing Group, Inc.

All rights reserved. No part of this book may be reproduced in any form or by any electronic or mechanical means, including information storage and retrieval systems, without written permission from the publisher, except by a reviewer who may quote passages in a review.

British Library Cataloguing in Publication Information Available

Library of Congress Cataloging-in-Publication Data

Names: Woody, Robert H. author.
Title: Becoming a real musician : inspiration and guidance for teachers and parents of musical kids / Robert H. Woody.
Description: Lanham : Rowman & Littlefield, [2019] | Includes bibliographical references and index.
Identifiers: LCCN 2019021133 (print) | LCCN 2019021780 (ebook) | ISBN 9781475849974 (Electronic) | ISBN 9781475849967 (cloth)
Subjects: LCSH: Music--Instruction and study--Parent participation. | Music--Instruction and study--Psychological aspects. | Child musicians--Psychology.
Classification: LCC MT1 (ebook) | LCC MT1 .W893 2019 (print) | DDC 780.71--dc23
LC record available at https://lccn.loc.gov/2019021133

To those who have musically and humanly inspired me most in my life, my wife, my parents, and my children.

CONTENTS

Preface		ix
1	Realness in Music	1
2	The Nature of Music	17
3	Motivation for Music	35
4	Creativity in Music	53
5	Improvisation of Music	67
6	Expressivity in Music	77
7	Performance of Music	97
8	The Humanness of Music	113
Index		127
About the Author		131

PREFACE

Contrary to my friends' quips about my "cushy job" as a music professor, I seem to keep pretty busy. Busy enough that I sometimes feel like I am just operating class to class, project to project, deadline to deadline. At such times, I have found it helpful to zoom out to look at the forest when I'm feeling trapped among the trees. Usually then I quickly remember how fortunate I am in my professional life to be in the company of some incredible musicians (my music faculty colleagues) and be inspired by the youthful enthusiasm of college kids studying music. Although I would deny that my job as a music professor is always "cushy," I cannot deny that it is a real blessing to be able to make a good living doing what I do.

The perspective afforded me by my professional position is but one source of the insights that have led to this book. I have also been fortunate enough to be the father of two children and stepfather to three more, all wonderfully musical in unique ways. With them I have played the role of music parent and attempted to apply my knowledge of music psychology and educational research. With mixed results! My experience with them has led to greater appreciation for adapting learning strategies to the individuality of learners. Another discovery has been the critical importance of a "teacher" being a "facilitator" and "encourager." And pursuant to this, I have learned that sometimes the best thing an adult can do is to stay out of the way and let a student's child-like love for music prevail.

I have been surprised by how much my perspective on music education has been informed by my experiences as a parent. Surprised and perhaps a little troubled, because the vast majority of people who enter the music teaching profession (usually as new college graduates) of course do so with no experience as parents. For this reason I am pleased to offer this book to both the teachers and parents of musical kids and I heartily encourage their collaboration so that their students' music learning will bring lifelong benefit.

In the spirit of giving credit where credit is due, I must also mention the time I have spent in K–12 American public schools, including a short but extremely enlightening stint as a full-time middle-school music teacher. There is nothing more "real world" or "on the front lines in the battle for the souls of our youth" than spending six to eight hours a day with hundreds of preteens! I have also gained insight into "keeping it real" musically by being a part of a small-town karaoke community. Special appreciation has come from watching my wife Angie shift from being a committed nonsinger (due to a "near death karaoke experience") to becoming an avid and accomplished karaoke performer. Karaoke singing has demonstrated how music can powerfully impact the lives of real people.

My everyday practical experiences as a parent, middle-school teacher, and karaoke enthusiast have helped to offset idealized dispositions I might adopt from spending most of my professional life in the ivory tower of higher education. For this reason I define a *real musician* not only as someone who is a music professional but also someone who makes music in a variety of real-life settings, including common social settings, from weddings and funerals to birthday parties and gatherings around a campfire.

I really started thinking about the term *real music* years ago when I came across some music education research in which school music students were contrasting the term "real music" against "school music."[1] Among kids, school music has been associated with difficult, analytical and passive lessons done with teacher-chosen style of music (usually classical, jazz, or similar), whereas "real music" brings to mind kid-preferred styles of music (popular styles), social interaction with friends, emotionally enjoyable experiences, and personal expression. It would of course be silly to try to exactly duplicate in formal education settings the informal social music experiences that kids prefer. Yet, learning would surely benefit (if only motivationally) from trying to make it more *real* for kids.

Just to be clear, I always have been and will remain a committed supporter of formal music education, such as through school music and private lessons. Every chance I get, I encourage parents to get their children involved in these time-tested institutions. I do, however, think music teachers can do more for students than they traditionally have, and parents should get more involved in the process too. As formal music learning has departed from the ways that human beings naturally make music, the harder it is for people to become musical. Over a half century ago, anthropologist Alan Merriam offered up a list of ten functions that music plays within human cultures around the world.[2] They are:

1. Emotional expression
2. Aesthetic enjoyment
3. Entertainment
4. Communication
5. Symbolic representation
6. Physical response
7. Enforcement of conformity to social norms
8. Validation of social institutions and religious rituals
9. Contribution to the continuity and stability of culture
10. Contribution to the integration of society

Merriam didn't offer these as a rank order, but I am heartened by seeing emotional expression at #1. In fact, it is likely that music is so effective with the other nine functions because it enhances them with its emotionally expressive capacity. For example, consider our American culture's passion for professional sports, NFL football in particular. This would likely be a "social institution" according to Merriam (college football is closer to a religious one!). Think about the many ways that music enhances our experience of NFL football: the stadium music, the enduring theme of Monday Night Football, and of course the Super Bowl halftime spectacles (U2 in 2002 was easily my all-time favorite).

Moving into the future, I expect that music education will evolve in ways that I seek to illuminate in this book. Each chapter offers a central theme or an avenue by which music learning for young people can be enhanced: Realness, Nature (of Music), Motivation, Creativity, Improvisation, Expressivity, Performance, and Humanness. In general, my perspective advocates for music teaching to become more inclusive and considerate of the learners themselves. As this evolution happens, parents will also have a critical role to play as facilitators.

NOTES

1. Graça M. Boal-Palheiros and David J. Hargreaves, "Listening to Music at Home and at School," *British Journal of Music Education* 18, no. 2 (2001): 103–18.

2. Alan P. Merriam, *The Anthropology of Music* (Chicago: Northwestern University Press, 1964).

1

REALNESS IN MUSIC

By and large, people love music. As an art form and as entertainment, music enhances life and gives people some of their most emotionally powerful and rewarding moments as human beings.

Also, by and large, people love children. Kids—from infancy to adolescence—have certain needs that must be met in order for them to develop well as human beings. They depend on adults to guide their developmental process. This is true from infancy, when they rely on adults for literally everything, to adolescence, when many youths refuse to acknowledge that they need adults for anything (but they do!). The key people in the lives of children, including in their musical lives, are their *parents*, their *teachers*, their *role models*. Kids' lives and their development into young adulthood is necessarily improved as they become more involved with music. Believing this is probably a precursor to reading this book.

Parents of children who are into music want them to get all they can out of their music activities, to be successful as music learners, have positive performance experiences, grow as people, and enjoy the rewards of the process for themselves. Most "music parents" don't *just hope* for these things for their kids, they are committed to them. They spend their money on the materials and experiences that a music education requires. They spend their time transporting their kids to lessons, rehearsal, and concerts. And they expend mental energy keeping track of what they're learning, convincing them to practice, and giving them emotional support along the way.

Music teachers, for their part, have made these things their life's work. Teaching is much more than a job. It's usually even more than an occupation. It's closer to a calling or a mission. Teachers are not just committed to the music education of their children, they're committed to the music education of *all* children.

When people give of themselves to support kids in music, they do it because they believe they're giving them a gift. It's perhaps one of the greatest gifts that can be given. Victor Hugo, author and poet of the Romantic era, eloquently stated, "Music expresses that which cannot be said and on which it is impossible to be silent."[1] More recently, singer-songwriter and piano man Billy Joel said, "Music in itself is healing. It's an explosive expression of humanity. It's something we are all touched by."[2] So music is not just a nice gift people give their kids like a hoped-for toy on their birthday, or even a high-quality useful gift that they really, really want, like brand-name jeans or an expensive bike. Music is a *powerful* gift. Giving the gift of music is among the most meaningful things adults can give their kids. It's akin to the values and life skills passed on through relationships with them.

A gift this nice shouldn't have an expiration date like a store gift card tucked in a wallet and forgotten about or pretty cut flowers in a vase that are slowly dying from the moment they're received. Music should be a gift that can last a lifetime.

Unfortunately, it seems that very few musically educated children grow up to become musically active adults. Too often the adults who oversee children's musical development are failing them. They are not giving them a gift with a lifetime warranty. Five, ten, or even fifteen years of instruction and experience may not equip them with musical skills and values that carry into adulthood, so they can be a creative and feelingful human beings who use music to express that which cannot be said but on which it is impossible to be silent. Most musically educated people, once in adulthood, are indistinguishable from those who received no music education as children. They're relegated to roles as mere consumers of music, who perhaps at times reminisce about their rewarding musical moments in childhood, much the way a former high-school sports standout wistfully recounts his "glory days" as a star athlete. Music should occupy a more meaningful role than this. Childhood nostalgia can be fun occasionally, but music education is capable of much more than just memory making.

The coming pages of this first chapter explain and illustrate what it means to be a real musician. Readers can expect to learn about these broad takeaway points:

- Largely due to its emotional and social rewards, musical involvement can be an extremely valuable gift to young people.
- Becoming a real musician means building the skills that support a musically active life.
- Although being musical lets many children feel special, the greatest contribution of music participation is allowing young people to feel real.

EXACTLY WHAT IS A "REAL MUSICIAN"?

Too often it turns out that the gift of a music education, given with such devotion and commitment by parents and teachers, does in fact have an expiration date. It ends rather abruptly when young people graduate from high school and start their adult lives. Many people have identified this dilemma. A number of researchers within the music education profession and the field of music psychology have studied this educational problem. For example, a husband and wife team of music educators once titled their research enterprise "Keeping Instruments Out of the Attic."[3] Others have issued the indictment that "those societies and communities with the most highly developed formal music education systems often appear to contain the least active music-making populations."[4] How can this be?

Another educational researcher, Dr. Susan O'Neill, has explained the problem as a matter of identity: "Even among children who play instruments and have instrumental music lessons, they do not necessarily incorporate their engagement in this activity as part of their self-concept." This explanation seems to fit kids whose parents provide them instruments and pay for extra music expenses and private lessons outside of school. These kids have been members of a school band, choir, or orchestra throughout their entire high-school education. But even these highly engaged musical kids rarely come to see themselves as musicians. Dr. O'Neill has explained, "This is often a result of the differences they observe between their own musical activities and those they associate with 'real' musicians in the adult world."[5]

In trying to pinpoint exactly what a "real musician" is, there are a variety of sources to consider. There are people who are inarguably musicians themselves, those for whom music is their vocation and their life's work. Relying on these people, however, is problematic since they are likely biased toward a definition of musician that includes music as profession. In addition, there is likely wide disagreement because the professional music world is vast and wildly diverse. Just consider the musical difference between a world-class classical violinist and freestyle rap artist!

If accepting opinions, an important thing to know is how kids themselves define what a real musician is. After all, it is kids who need to be reached and convinced that they too can have "musician" as part of their self-concept. Researchers have in fact examined kids' definitions of "real musician." Not surprisingly, they've found a wide variety of opinions. And although kids are not in perfect agreement about what a real musician *is*, they seem to agree quite a lot about what one *is not*. Even active music participants consider themselves "nonmusicians" because they see what they do in music education as the same as what they believe "real" musicians do.[5] So whatever a "real musician" does, kids do not see that as part of their own music learning experiences.

To be more direct, a *real musician* is someone whose musical skill set enables him or her to lead a musically active life, whether music making is their paid profession or is an avocation for their leisure time.

Deciding exactly what a real musician is requires consideration of some definitions and descriptions of the word *real*. These can be easily applied to music making and helpful in deciding what a person needs to become a real musician. The "real world" is the realm of practical or actual experience, as opposed to the abstract, theoretical, or idealized sphere of the laboratory or classroom. And according to the *Cambridge Advanced Learner's Dictionary and Thesaurus*, the phrase "Get real!" tells people that they should try to understand the true facts of a situation and not hope for what is impossible.

The musical adults in children's lives need to *get real* about what they want them to get out of the music educational opportunities and musical-social experiences they give them. The goal of this book is *not* to reveal what young people must do to acquire the skills of a professional musician, or how to make a good living as a performer. A "real musician" is best defined as someone who is able to participate in music making in a variety of real-life settings, including common social situations: from large formal gatherings such as weddings and funerals to smaller informal ones such as a circle of friends and family around a campfire. "Real musicians" effectively use their performance to do what music is designed to primarily do: share expressions of humanness through the artistic styling of sound.

LEARNING MUSIC VS. REAL MUSIC

Pop culture is sometimes very revealing. Although pop culture is often dominated by celebrities and the entertainment industry and may not seem "real world" for many people, it is a good indication of who they *really* are. What people make popular—with their time and attention to various media, with their clicks online, and with the spending of their disposable income—says a lot about who they are as people. And pop culture is surely influential in the experiences of people's lived real worlds.

Every year when the Super Bowl arrives, music takes center stage. Granted, it shares the stage with football and television ads and sometimes politics. But music is a huge part of the Super Bowl experience. And one of the biggest Super Bowl spectacles in recent memory was in 2014. After its conclusion, most people agreed that the music of that year's Super Bowl was much better than the football game itself. The music included a wonderful breadth of style. The multitalented Queen Latifah sang "America the Beautiful," operatic superstar Renée Fleming performed the National Anthem, and viewers were treated to a lively halftime pairing of Bruno Mars and the Red Hot Chili Peppers.

Following Ms. Fleming's breathtaking performance, viewers' opinions about her anthem performance poured in on social media. Many praised her rendition, but there was another particular perspective offered by some of the most highly trained musicians and people in the music education profession. Some of these people said things to the effect of: "For once we got to hear the anthem sung by a *real singer.*" Maybe this sentiment is just the letting off of steam by formally trained musicians who are frustrated that their preferred styles are not more present in pop culture. But instead of referring to the anthem's operatic stylings as "my kind of music" or even "good music," some people suggested that they finally got to hear some *"real music."*

Clearly many in the world of formal music education consider classical music (or maybe jazz) to be the most meaningful, exemplary, and *real* music there is. This perspective, however, is most definitely not shared by the vast majority of people in Western society. This includes the kids in schools. Research has confirmed that in the minds of most young people, there can be a significant disconnect between their conceptions of school music and what they consider to be real music.[6] For music educators, this disconnect is more than just a nuisance, or a mark of immaturity that must be overcome. Learning of any kind is greatly influenced by students' intrinsic motivation for the subject matter and their beliefs about its relevance to their lives.

People in music education could benefit from looking at how people learn and value music in the real world and from incorporating those insights into teaching activities. Constructivist theory in education says that people learn best through active involvement with their environments. Especially important for children are collaborative experiences with other kids and adults. This is because human beings instinctively observe what others do and attempt to reproduce it themselves. Young people desire opportunities to experiment with music (including freely making mistakes), to be creative and expressive with it, and to find personal meaning in it.[7] When these characteristics are present in school music activities, students of all ages are more likely to see their learning experiences as "real music."

Research suggests that many adolescents see music lessons (like classes in other subjects) as undertakings done to satisfy teachers and parents. School music is often linked to the performance of nonpreferred styles, using an analytical approach, and difficult or boring teaching sessions. Keep in mind, of course, that this broad perspective does not represent only the students who have found a home in the school band, choir, or orchestra, but the comparative majority who elect not to take any music in secondary school. In contrast, adolescents associate *real music* with popular and familiar styles, using a subjective and emotional approach, which usually takes place in relaxed and fun settings with others. This conception of real music is much closer to that held by most people around the world. They turn to music for the emotional rewards it provides, and it is very often a part of deeply meaningful social interactions among people.

As alluded to above, this disconnect between formal music education and real music can cause many students to avoid music learning opportunities altogether when school music offerings become elective courses. And for the students who do elect to do school music, many carry on musical "double lives" that prevent them from getting the most out of their childhood music experiences. Even some who go on to become music teachers were, as a teenagers, prime examples of this. They played a band or orchestra instrument in school ensembles, but outside of school, they were heavy consumers of popular music (and even today, it's the pop music of their youth that fills the music apps on their smartphones!). What's more, the musical divide was not simply a matter of stylistic genre. Musicianship in school was limited to playing just one instrument, almost always from notation, and in preparation for a public performance. Out-of-school musicality was also quite limited, but in very different ways. It included listening and singing along to recordings, either alone or with friends, but never for an audience. Such conflicted existences are surely had by many of today's best young music students.

Of course it would be foolish to suggest that teachers, parents, and students are doing it all wrong in formal music education, or that schools should try to reproduce exactly in music lessons what informal experiences provide so naturally in kids' social lives. It is, however, just as foolish for music teachers and parents to dismiss kids' preferred styles of popular music as somehow less real or worthy of consideration. Pop, rock, hip-hop, country, rap, and other styles make up the *native* music of the students. In a pluralistic and democratic society, people's native cultures are to be accepted, appreciated, and celebrated; this orientation is what allows people to find identity and a sense of belonging, and to thrive in life. And the importance of popular music to teenagers is as strong as the most identifying cultural trait is to any ethnic group or community of people. Popular music being the native music of kids should not be a reason to ignore it—native English-speaking children are required to take English classes throughout the entirety of their schooling—but a reason to respect it. It's also important to acknowledge people's natural orientation to music, that is, the appeal it has through personal relevance, emotional investment, and social interaction. These experiences are not only part of *natural musicality*, they also can contribute to *efficient learning*.⁸

MUSICAL KIDS—FINDING IDENTITY AND AUTHENTICITY

It is no wonder that music can play such a significant role in the lives of children and teenagers. After all, kids are people too. Human beings have always enjoyed music, and there has never been a time in history when so much of it is so readily available to so many people. Although music has always been important to people, today it may be the most important it's ever been in the lives of people all around the world.

The research of psychologists and sociologists has confirmed humanity's love affair with music. People interact with music both alone and with others, and in both private and public settings. Having choice in the music they listen to or perform is critical, in part because people primarily love music for its connection to emotion and mood.

Music is also a favorite material for human beings to use in forming an *identity*, which typically goes into high gear in middle childhood and adolescence. During the teen years, most youths gain a sense of who they are. This complex process involves internalizing role models, from family, other adults, and admired peers. Their unique musical experiences, and the strong emotions they evoke, also contribute to identity development.

When young people are on that identity quest, and trying to figure out "who I am," they are indeed looking for something, even though they may not know exactly what. Involvement with music can be a part of their finding an important something. It can help them to feel like they've learned something about who they really are. Music can appeal to kids for a variety of reasons, and what they take from the involvement is unique.

Music participation can meet an important need of childhood and adolescence, in that *it allows kids to feel special*. This benefit is most often readily linked to traditional music lessons and traditional school music opportunities. Early in a child's music experience, when everything is new, moments of feeling special abound. You feel special having a shiny silver band instrument. You feel special taking your position on stage on the risers with the other robed choir members. If, as a beginning violinist, you can scratch out something that sounds the least bit like "Hot Cross Buns," you feel special as parents and teacher smile and show that they recognize the tune. But feeling special can be a double-edged sword. When the newness of the experience has worn off and praise is not as easily collected, when practice time is required to learn to play the assigned music and still there seems to be students who are better performers than you, then the feeling of specialness may fade. Even students who end up being among the best of their peers and retain a sense of specialness throughout adolescence may not give music a permanent place in their identity. In other words, it does not stay for the rest of their lives.

Another way that music participation meets a need of childhood and adolescence is that *it allows young people to feel connected to others*. It is well documented that organized music participation is a popular means by which young people engage in social bonding. This happens as they share the experiences of rehearsing and performing together, and spend time traveling to special events and on group trips. Membership in school and community music groups presents settings in which young people can easily find friends with similar interests, feel a sense of belonging to a close-knit group or "family" of musicians, and even find romance.[9]

As explained above, the experiences that come with music involvement allow students to feel special and to feel connected to others. While such positive feelings contribute to a healthy childhood and proper human development, these feelings and their benefits are not unique to music. They can be had by youths who excel in sports, who are involved in a church or community groups, or who are strong academic achievers in school. Also, that feeling special and feeling connected are *not* the best that music has to offer. Such feelings alone are not often effective at turning kids into life-long music makers as adults. *The most powerful contribution of musical participation to the needs of children and adolescents is that it can allow them to feel real.*

MAKING MUSIC LEARNING MORE REAL

Though some modern realities can paint a bleak picture of young people's musical prospects today, this book's purpose is not just to shine a spotlight on poor practices and undesirable outcomes that exist in music teaching and learning. There are some problems that need to be addressed to be sure, but kids today have the potential to be more musical than any generation before them. They will not reach their potential of becoming real musicians unless the adults in their lives do a better job in how they serve and support them along the way.

The key to achieving this goal does not involve some revolutionary approach that's been newly invented. Far from it, what's offered in this book simply synthesizes preexisting sound ideas and research. It does not espouse any particular teaching methodology or the ideas of any one pedagogue. Instead, much insight can be gained just by looking at the way that people are naturally musical. While this may sound like a loaded statement, here's what it means. If the problem is that music teaching in schools and private lessons has become too impractical, too specialized, and generally not real enough, then a solution is apparent: look at how people have done and continue to do music throughout history and all around the world. Contrary to the common sentiment, music is not a universal language. But there are some commonalities about how people do music across cultural lines. These are *naturally human* if not universal.

The phrase "naturally human" is a great descriptor of music when it's at its best. In fact, to pinpoint just one single strategy for music teaching to improve its effectiveness with young people: it needs to incorporate into instruction and learning activities more of what is naturally human about making music. But what exactly does this mean?

The ideas about what is natural and human about music serve as bookends for the rest of this book (chapters 2 through 8). Between these bookends are other critical concepts that make music learning meaningful and lasting. Each of the remaining chapters in this book focuses on one quality of music making that makes it *real*. Kids are most likely to become *real musicians* when their instruction and learning experiences encompass the following principles:

Reflect the True Nature of Music

Sometimes supporters of the arts can too easily get caught up in justifying music study by its likely contribution to other skills such as abstract reasoning, language acquisition, and self-discipline. While these possible "transfer effects" of music are enticing to use with people who just don't "get it" from an arts standpoint, there is not compelling research that studying music makes kids smarter or have better moral character. But this is certain: proper study of music will make kids *more musical*. And that should be compelling enough for anyone who's experienced the power of music at some point in life. Chapter 2, "The Nature of Music," explores the most significant qualities *at the heart* of human music making. The closer music experiences stay to these defining characteristics, the more obvious it is to everyone that becoming *more musical* is a life-enriching pursuit that can be enjoyed by all people.

Motivate Kids in a Variety of Meaningful Ways

People often talk about motivation as if it's merely a feeling that overcomes them. Just as many would-be fitness buffs struggle with not "being motivated" to go to the gym, young musicians often complain of not being motivated to practice and engage in the activities that will improve their musical skills. What they're really saying is they just *don't feel like* going to work out or practice their instrument. Many music students are seemingly content to wait (and wait . . . and wait . . .) until they do *feel like it* before doing what they should. Chapter 3, "Motivation in Music," surveys the complete nature of motivation. It covers ways to structure the optimal music learning environment and other extrinsic sources of motivation, and explain how to tap into the most effective intrinsic motivators for young people.

Allow for Creativity

Because music is an art, and the arts are one of humankind's primary means of being creative, people often credit music study for developing students' creative thinking. It's hard to deny, however, that formal music study in schools and private studios leaves little opportunity for students to handle music creatively. One reason is that most formal music making is focused on performing the published works of professional composers. And many teachers resist giving their students composing or songwriting experiences for themselves for fear that such attention will take away valuable time from the paramount goal of "performing the repertoire." Giving young people creative experiences with music does take time, but it is certainly not time wasted. Chapter 4, "Creativity in Music," demystifies creativity and shows that all people are capable of being creative with music. Although a young musician may not compose symphonies like Beethoven or win a Nobel Prize in Literature like songwriter Bob Dylan, having opportunities to artistically express one's most personal thoughts will *make music more real* for anyone.

Include Improvising

You may associate improvisation with a very limited number of musical contexts, probably jazz and maybe guitar solos in rock and roll. But improvising was more commonplace in all Western music before print notation of music became so technologically easy (think printing press proliferation in the nineteenth century) at which time classical music began its devotion to and dependence on notation for virtually all performance. And worldwide—outside of formal/classical music circles—improvisation remains a staple in human music making. Chapter 5, "Improvisation of Music," shows how young musicians who learn to improvise feel especially *empowered* by it. That is, they are able to readily adapt and at least *do something musical* in any context, even with music material they don't know well and with other musicians with whom they've never rehearsed or performed before.

Emphasize Emotional Expression and Communication

Although music is not a universal language, it is a powerful medium by which people communicate feelings to one another. Research has shown that music can effectively convey broad emotions or moods such as joy or sadness, and many great musical minds have advanced the idea of its ineffability—that music can express some of the subtleties and complexities of human emotion even more precisely than words. Chapter 6, "Expressivity in Music," first tackles the basic question of how music communicates meaning to listeners, then considers the processes through which performers translate their emotional intentions into sounded music. The chapter also looks at other factors that affect the emotional experience that audience members may have at a live musical performance.

Keep Performance in Proper Perspective

Ideally, student musicians approach performance with the goal of simply sharing their music with heartfelt expression that will emotionally move their listeners. Truth be told, however, this probably happens far too infrequently in school auditoriums and recital halls. Sometimes the only emotion young musicians bring to performance is fear, as stage fright takes hold. Whether students' experiences on stage are marked by moving expressivity or debilitating stage fright can be influenced by the way they are taught to think of performance. Is it simple sharing or a high-stakes special presentation that should impress those in the audience? Chapter 7, "Performance of Music," will shed light on the music-killing problem of performance anxiety, and show that the best way to solve the problem is to avoid it altogether by helping young musicians choose their goals realistically, and to plan, prepare, and practice for performances wisely.

Prioritize What Is Most Human about Music

Without proper perspective, music teachers can focus too much on helping students with the details of performing the right notes with the best technique. Parents can get preoccupied with encouraging their kids to practice and celebrating their performance achievements. There is a danger of losing sight of the big picture. Perhaps adults' critical role is to promote the connection between *being musical* and *being human*. For young musicians-in-training to become *real musicians*, perhaps in addition to learning a lot about music, they need to learn something about human beings. After all, it is *people* who make up the audiences whose emotions musicians strive to stir. And of course for most musicians, the most rewarding music-making experiences are those in which they meaningfully share the stage—or the recording studio, or the garage, or the circle around the campfire—with other musicians. Chapter

8, "The Humanness of Music," drives home the biggest takeaway from this book: not only should all *humans make music*, perhaps more importantly, *music makes people human*.

NOTES

1. Victor Hugo, *William Shakespeare* (London: Hauteville, 1864), 73.
2. Ken Bielen, *The Words and Music of Billy Joel* (Santa Barbara, CA: Praeger, 2011), 2.
3. Dan Isbell and Ann Marie Stanley, "Keeping Instruments Out of the Attic: The Concert Band Experiences of the Non-Music Major," *Music Education Research International* 5, no. 1 (2011): 22–33.
4. Lucy Green, *How Popular Musicians Learn: A Way Ahead for Music Education* (Aldershot, UK: Ashgate, 2002), 5.
5. Susan A. O'Neill, "The Self-Identity of Young Musicians," in *Musical Identities*, edited by Raymond A. R. MacDonald, David J. Hargreaves, and Dorothy Meill, 79–96 (Oxford: Oxford University Press, 2002), 85.
6. Research identifying a disconnect between school music and "real music" include: Graça M. Boal-Palheiros and David J. Hargreaves, "Listening to Music at Home and at School," *British Journal of Music Education* 18, no. 2 (2001): 103–08; David J. Hargreaves and Nigel A. Marshall, "Developing Identities in Music Education," *Music Education Research* 5, no. 3 (2003): 263–74; and Alexandra Lamont, David J. Hargreaves, Nigel A. Marshall, and Mark Tarrant, "Young People's Music In and Out of School," *British Journal of Music Education* 20, no. 3 (2003): 229–41.
7. Patricia Shehan Campbell, Claire Connell, and Amy Beegle, "Adolescents' Expressed Meanings of Music in and out of School," *Journal of Research in Music Education* 55, no. 3 (2007): 220–36.
8. Gianna G. Cassidy and Anna M. J. M. Paisley, "Music-games: A Case Study of Their Impact," *Research Studies in Music Education* 35, no. 1 (2013): 119–38.
9. Research confirming the social bonding had by kids in school music groups include: Melissa Arasi, "The Lifelong Impact of the Choral Experience: Philosophy and Teaching Styles," in *The School Choral Program: Philosophy, Planning, Organizing, and Teaching*, edited by Michele Holt and James Jordan, 1–42 (Chicago: GIA, 2008); Campbell, Connell, and Beegle, "Adolescents' Expressed Meanings of Music in and out of School"; Cecil Adderley, Mary Kennedy, and William Berz, "'A Home Away from Home': The World of the High School Music Classroom," *Journal of Research in Music Education* 51, no. 3 (2003): 190–205; and Elizabeth Cassidy Parker, "Exploring Student

Experiences of Belonging within an Urban High School Choral Ensemble: An Action Research Study," *Music Education Research* 12, no. 4 (2010): 339–52.

2

THE NATURE OF MUSIC

Talking about the nature of music is a tricky task indeed, largely because music is so vast and varied. With *so many* different kinds of music, people who write and talk about music for a living try to mitigate the confusion by applying categorical labels and descriptors. Even so, the meaning of the most commonly used terms can be quite problematic. For example, how can someone's favorite "pop" musicians be those who are not popular, and how is it that there's new "classical" music being composed every day? And what can be made of the terms "world music" (as if there's some music out there that's *not* part of the world) and "alternative music" (alternative to *what* exactly?)?

Accordingly, this chapter's consideration of the nature of music starts off by conceding that there really is no *single* nature that applies to all music. What is natural, normal, and genuine in, say, the field of classical music is not so in the more popular genres of rock, pop, hip-hop, R&B, and country. That said, it is possible to talk meaningfully about human musical experience in a general context and draw some conclusions about the nature of music. This approach supports the overall goal of understanding how to make music *real* for kids.

The previous chapter closed by suggesting that young musicians-in-training may be more likely to become *real musicians* if, in addition to learning a lot about music, they learn some important things about human beings. Thomas Turino is one of the best musical thinkers of today because he knows a great deal about both music and human beings. A professor of musicology and anthropology, Dr. Turino begins his fine book *Music as Social Life* with a discussion of *why music matters*. He supports his assertion that musical sounds are a "powerful human resource" in that they are often at the heart of people's most profound occasions and experiences:

> People in societies around the world use music to create and express their emotional inner lives, to span the chasm between themselves and the divine, to woo lovers, to celebrate weddings, to sustain friendships and communities, to inspire mass political movements, and to help their babies fall asleep.[1]

Anthropology, as a field of study, has long looked to people's uses of music to understand humankind and its cultures. Dr. Turino's examples above show that music is a veritable constant in everyday life. Around the world it is commonplace for people to use music to regulate their moods and emotions (e.g., to match and maintain a good mood or "repair" a bad mood), to help pass the time when at work, to enrich social interactions, and to affirm their identities to themselves and others around them.

Please note the kind of the language used thus far in this chapter. The idea of people *using* music has come up repeatedly, and terms like "every day," "normal," and "commonplace" have appeared throughout. What is musically natural is best understood as what is normal, native, and typically done by people. To know the *nature of music* one must look at how people do music and use music in their natural settings, that is, the contexts that are ordinary and functional for people, rather than those that are artificial, formal, or prefabricated.

The aforementioned musicologist/anthropologist Tom Turino likes to divide the world of music not into style genres or categories offered by the music industry, but by *fields* based on how and why people do music as they do. Along these lines, music performance can be divided into *presentational* performance and *participatory* performance. North American music education, borrowing from the conventions and values of Western classical music, has long been entrenched in the presentational performance field. While this emphasis has produced a long tradition of impressive concerts and remarkable travel opportunities and performance experiences for students, an unfortunate byproduct seems to be an epidemic of music "graduates" who are not particularly musical

THE NATURE OF MUSIC

in their adult lives. Perhaps music students would benefit from a move toward the participatory performance field.

As its title indicates, this chapter focuses on the nature of music. Readers can look for these major points:

- The true nature of music is revealed in the ways people do music and use music in their natural settings, that is, the functional contexts of people's ordinary lives.
- Music making is most natural when it allows for expressive spontaneity and when it is participatory rather than presentational.
- Even in situations where music seems to be "mere entertainment" it still offers people opportunity to meaningfully connect to others and to get in touch with their humanness.

WRITING KIDS' SUCCESS STORIES

To avoid delving too deeply into the weeds of music philosophy, some storytelling can effectively convey how all this relates to kids. The three young people named below are not real individuals—notice they have alliterative names—but they are based on real kids. Please read the following three vignettes carefully because they will be referenced in the rest of this chapter that follows. It is likely that at least one of them will remind you of someone you know, perhaps a music student of yours, a child of one of your friends, or maybe even yourself in the past.

Vincent the Valedictorian Violinist

Born to parents who greatly valued achievement of all kinds, Vincent inherited their philosophy, "If it's worth doing, it's worth doing successfully." Academic and artistic achievement were given much priority. Young Vincent started violin lessons even before he started preschool, though with the amount of reading his parents did with him as a toddler, his home life was almost school-like. Classical music was favored by his parents because they believe it instilled discipline and appreciation for excellence, values that were also reinforced through Vincent's tae-kwon-do classes (he earned a black belt at age fifteen) and in his pursuit for straight As on every report card. As a high-school senior,

Vincent targeted Ivy League schools for college and planned to study a STEM field (STEM stands for Science, Technology, Engineering, and Mathematics). Even though he could have filled his high-school schedule with extra Advanced Placement classes and occupied his after-school time exclusively with the school robotics club, he remained committed to the school orchestra, as well as pursuing solo violin accomplishments through private lessons. This commitment to music earned him the praise and gratitude of the school orchestra teacher, who rewarded Vincent by naming him senior soloist for the final orchestra concert of the year. Although he enjoyed his music activities in high school, he knew that "extracurriculars" were mostly important for looking "well rounded" and showing and "artistic/creative side," this quality being appraised favorably by college admissions officers and future employers in the corporate world.

When Vincent went to college (yes, in the Ivy League), he had his violin with him, at least for his freshman year. Later, conceding that he no longer had time to join an orchestra, he had no reason to play the instrument. His violin in his dorm room became an unpleasant reminder of how much time he spent studying it all through childhood only to end up with it having no meaningful role in his new life as an adult. Occasionally, however, his friends would see it there and make him pull it out and play for them. Every time this happened, he played the only thing he remembered, the piece from his final high-school orchestra concert as "senior soloist." When someone asked him if he could fiddle some bluegrass music (which happened surprisingly often), he would quickly put the instrument away, and get back to homework.

Taylor the Team-Player Trumpeter

Like most of her friends at the time, Taylor signed up for the school band in fifth grade. With parents pushing her, Taylor thought being in the band with her friends would be fun. Her parents favored the idea of "band kids" being Taylor's social group in middle and high school. Taylor figured she'd stick with it as long as she enjoyed it and her friends were in it. By the time she got into high school, Taylor was a pretty good trumpet player. The high-school band director showed support and much appreciation for her involvement in the band. Having been in the school band for about five years, she felt a connection to it, and it didn't hurt that her boyfriend was a committed band member too. Although she was bored at times with rehearsals and occasionally resented that band activities prevented her from doing other enjoyable things, being in the band gave her a sense of belonging and the band room felt like a home away from home. Taylor sensed that as a full-fledged "band kid" now, her social standing was secured by her trumpet success. Consequently, she practiced her instrument at home to assure that she'd sound good at the next rehearsal or concert. In her junior year, she was named a trumpet section leader and started to feel a real sense of responsibility, not only for her own effort in band, but for that of her fellow trumpeters. As a high-school senior, she became one of the most committed student leaders in the entire band program and a personal contributor to the group's exceptional success that year.

After high school, Taylor went to college at a large state university where she majored in business management with a minor in psychology (even though her high-school band director insisted that she was "good enough to be a music major in college"). She was in the university's marching band during her first semester in college, but dropped it after her freshman year because membership in the college marching band just didn't measure up to her "awesome" experience in high school. Following graduation from college, Taylor went on to become a rising star in the corporate world, and she often credited her school band experience with teaching her a strong work ethic, people skills, and a leadership orientation.

Sophie the Soulful Songstress

Being the youngest in a family with three children was sometimes frustrating for Sophie, but she also enjoyed certain advantages in this role. For example, when her mother took Sophie to her older sister Hallie's piano lessons, while Hallie sat on the piano bench with the teacher and Mom sat off to the side dutifully taking notes, Sophie sat by her mother holding whatever toy she'd been given. However, with Sophie listening intently in the lesson, it was not long before Sophie began trying to play for herself the music that her big sister was working on. At first Hallie thought it was cute that baby sister Sophie was trying to mimic her music making, but at some point, Sophie's piano performance skills came close to matching Hallie's. Because of Sophie's clear interest in music and the fact that she was able to learn piano from just hearing her sister's lessons, the family began commenting on Sophie's "knack for" music. (Hallie did not find that at all cute.)

Sophie eventually took piano lessons herself and started on cello in her elementary school's orchestra program in fourth grade. But by the time Sophie was heading into high school she was pleading with her parents to let her quit orchestra. There were a number of other activities that demanded her time that were more important than orchestra rehearsals and cello practice; these included the speech and debate team, volleyball, and social time with friends. Her debate prowess helped convince her parents to let her drop cello, and in what was almost a response of desperation, her dad presented Sophie with a ukulele for her fourteenth birthday so she could at least maintain some musical connection in her life. Sophie took to the uke like a fish to water. Using YouTube and other websites, Sophie quickly learned how to accompany herself singing her favorite popular songs. Within months she had used her birthday and Christmas gift money to buy herself a guitar.

Playing the guitar was nothing like the battle Mom and Dad once had getting Sophie to practice cello. In fact, they sometimes had to remind her to take a break from guitar to get homework done or to be on time for plans she had made with friends. In high school, Sophie made some videos clips of herself performing songs and put them out on social media. Her followers—mostly friends and acquaintances from school and church—praised her profusely for them and practically demanded more. Sophie and her guitar were also a hit for impromptu sing-alongs at sleepovers with friends and around campfires at church youth-group outings.

As a young adult, Sophie happily offered her guitar accompaniment and song leading abilities to church worship services, and to family get-togethers large and small. As adult life happened to Sophie, she turned to her music to express the powerful emotions she felt from falling in love, the birth of her children, and the sorrowful loss of loved ones. She sometimes played and sang for an audience, but just as often she made music by herself for herself.

Morals of the Stories

Perhaps one of these stories reminded you of someone you know. Those accounts describe some very common types of kids' involvement in music. Now here's a question that highlights the main purpose of the stories of Vincent, Taylor, and Sophie: which of the three vignettes would you call a musical success story?

Clearly music was a very positive factor in the lives of all three of the kids. Both Vincent the valedictorian violinist and Taylor the team-player trumpeter had very good school-music experiences. In part, due to the support they received from the adults in their lives, they came to value music education for themselves and became self-motivated to do school music and take private lessons. They stayed in music through the entirety of their schooling, and later credited their musical experiences for contributing to their early successes as adults: Vincent getting into an Ivy League school, and Taylor becoming a star manager in the corporate world.

Although Vincent's and Taylor's are stories of successful kids, they cannot be called *musical* success stories. While both had good school music experiences and participated through high school, their music education did not succeed in equipping and motivating them to be musically active as adults.

What did Sophie's musical childhood accomplish that Vincent's and Taylor's did not? Sophie's musical interactions enabled her to experience the true nature of music. As alluded to earlier, what is musically natural is best determined by considering how human beings have done and continue to do music throughout history and all around the world. This notion differs from simply starting with the music tradition that is most commonplace, labeling it the best, and adopting it as what all kids should do.

It could easily be said that Vincent's and Taylor's *good* music education was *not good enough*. It was not good enough to prepare them for a musical adulthood. Education in any subject should ultimately equip learners with an *independence* for managing and applying the knowledge and skills they've acquired. Though Vincent and Taylor were relatively accomplished as music students, they did not develop musical independence. Some degree of independence is needed for people to personally integrate music making into that which is normal, commonplace, and done in the natural settings of their lives. Only then can they experience what is musically natural.

The music making of Vincent and Taylor included a marked *dependence*—in fact, a cynic might call it codependence. Even at the height of their musical involvement, Vincent and Taylor relied on a teacher and the organized system of school music and formal lessons to define all of their music making. Their teacher chose the music for them to play, and provided the sheet music which told them what notes to play. They depended on teacher-run rehearsals and lessons for instruction about how to play the chosen music, and on the teacher-scheduled concert or recital for motivation to practice and the opportunity to performance. Without a teacher and a formal system in place, Vincent and Taylor were essentially *unable* to do any music making on their own.

To complicate matters further, sometimes a music education like the one received by Vincent and Taylor, despite its inbuilt dependence, can give the impression that it was very good for students—perhaps even *too good*. Recall that Taylor's experiences with the school band were so emotionally and socially gratifying that as an adult, through the nostalgic lens of childhood, she felt that music making could never be that good again. So why bother trying?

BORROWING FROM VERNACULAR MUSICIANSHIP

Referring back to the vignettes above, recall that Sophie's youthful music-making experiences ultimately found a place in her identity, such that she was able and motivated to make music in meaningful ways in her adult life. She was the beneficiary of formal music education, both in terms of receiving private lessons (in fact, she got something of a "double dose" from sitting in on her older sister's lessons!) and being in elementary- and middle-school orchestras. These organized experiences, however, did not comprise the entire context of her music making. Rather, Sophie was afforded opportunity to explore her own personal musical tastes (favorite popular songs) and incorporate her music making into the natural settings of her life (in her case social media and informal gatherings with friends). Or as a result, she identified broadly with the nature of music, as she felt the powerful social and emotional rewards of self-expressive music making.

Clearly Sophie's trajectory into guitar playing, sing-alongs, and songwriting departed from traditional formal music education. Many people who have existed exclusively in the musical confines of formal education may look at informal music makers and "garage band" musicians with some bewilderment. Maybe even with a little disdain. How is it that these guitarists, electric bassists, and drummers learn their instruments, often without the assistance of music teachers? They can figure out so much, seemingly on their own. But if they've done it without instruction from a musical expert, doesn't that call into question the quality of their skills?

Back in 2002, music educator and researcher Lucy Green published her book *How Popular Musicians Learn*. Lucy was not the first scholar to study the processes of "rock band" musicians, but she was one of the first to offer an entire book on it. The subtitle of her book directly stated the promise she thought her work offered: *A Way Ahead for Music Education*.[2] The book shed light on the learning processes of "vernacular musicians," as they're sometimes called, who acquire their musicianship outside of a school/lesson setting. Lucy and others continued with additional research further exploring the topic. Lately, many within the music education profession have been paying greater attention to vernacular musicians. Scholars have found that these people do not devote any less time and energy to their musical pursuits than those in more formal settings. Research refutes the notion that popular music skills are arrived at by osmosis (through just goofing around with music), whereas good "classical" musicianship comes through discipline. More likely, the real difference is whether the time and effort invested is perceived as pleasant or unpleasant. Most vernacular musicians describe their music activities as voluntary, enjoyable, and what they love to do. They seem to tap into more intrinsic motivation than many formally trained students, whose music experiences can be dominated by solitary technique-intensive practice of music assigned to them by teachers.

It's interesting to note that virtually everyone starts off as a vernacular musician. Most people first learn everything through enculturation, that is, through immersion in their native culture and social environment. Young children begin learning music as they're exposed to music making around them and naturally engage in playful exploration of musical sound. But upon reaching schooling age, some people become invested in formal music instruction, and their music-making activities take on that value system. Much of their time is spent in teacher-led lessons and rehearsals, and in solitary practice sessions. Young vernacular musicians, however, typically continue on a more exploratory path. Below are some of the most important characteristics of vernacular music learning:

- Informal group learning with peers. A more experienced peer may lead informal sessions, sharing previously unfamiliar chords, progressions, or licks. In less-directed peer situations, learning is accomplished as musicians engage in group efforts to reproduce popular songs, create new compositions or arrangements, and otherwise jam for pure enjoyment.
- Chosen musical material. Practicing is done within a real music context. That is, emphasis is on songs, tunes, or licks that they want to learn, as opposed to teacher-assigned scales, long-tones, and exercises. Interestingly though, many vernacular musicians eventually choose to practice scales, arpeggios, and other exercises as they "discover" the benefits, often through suggestions published in musician magazines and on online musician discussion boards.
- Listening-copying process. They often "just listen" to soak up a groove, or try to play along with recordings for fun. But they also thrive on the challenge of listening carefully and working up imitative performances of difficult passages.

Obviously the ear is a critical component for vernacular musicians. It is the means by which they build up a huge repertoire of songs, quickly memorize heard music, embellish basic music material, and improvise. In contrast to formally trained music students who rely greatly on notation in their practicing, vernacular musicians naturally develop formidable aural skills as they practice.

This line of thinking should in no way discredit the value of having a great music teacher or the effectiveness of individual practice. The research literature is replete with evidence that formal education works and that deliberate practice leads to improved skills. But surely the activities of vernacular musicians have something to contribute to music education.

"Vernacular" is a good descriptor for this kind of musicianship because vernacular is defined as that which is native, ordinary, and everyday. Applied to the field of architecture, vernacular refers to structures that are functional rather than monumental, in other words, that which is natural, rather than artificial, formal, or fabricated.

Chapter 1 discussed a few ways that music participation can meet important needs of childhood and adolescence. The first was that *it allows kids to feel special*. While this is a good and valuable contribution of music, it is not the best benefit. Even the students who maintain that "special" feeling throughout high school (like Vincent and Taylor in the above vignettes), often do not incorporate music into a permanent facet of their identity.

ENTERTAINMENT IS NOT JUST ENTERTAINMENT

Well-intentioned music educators can rely too much on the "specialness" benefit of music participation. They may see this argument as getting music its due respect among other "core" subjects like math, English, and science. Arts advocates resent that the subject of music gets relegated to the status of a frill. In other words, many schools treat music as an extracurricular or enrichment activity for students. Or they may see school music merely as the means for providing entertainment for school assemblies, sporting events, and occasional concerts.

As music teachers have continued efforts to make their students' performances more special, impressive, and publicly appreciated, they have simultaneously argued that music is not just entertainment. While this point is true and should be made to school administrators, parents, and student musicians themselves, music advocates must also be careful how they go about refuting the perspective of "music as mere entertainment."

Unfortunately in efforts to defend the place of music in children's education, some supporters stray from the true nature of music by emphasizing its contributions to other skills such as abstract reasoning, language acquisition, math proficiency, self-discipline, and spatial intelligence. Many otherwise proud members of the music education profession are terribly embarrassed when hearing music teachers boast that "music makes you smarter," or that it produces more conscientious and productive members of society. Although such transfer effects do exist (some of them anyway), they do not make for a compelling argument. For example, if a child is struggling with math, will thoughtful parents' response be to find more music opportunities for her? More likely, they'll look to get her some better math instruction. Also note that math teachers do not justify their subject's place in a school curriculum by its contributions to students' self-discipline and interpersonal skills. Math is a staple in the curriculum because most believe that the subject matter itself is important for everyone.

Defenders of school music would do well to promote the value of music based on its own merits. And its merits mainly have to do with the powerful nature of music to human beings. The main purpose of music—like all the arts—is expression. The importance of music is best seen in its unique ability to provide people with a means of exercising creativity and self-expression. Advocates of music education should focus on this unique benefit. If they adopt this defense of music, however, those in the profession must then be sure to teach in a way that truly gives students opportunities to be creative and express themselves. In many cases, this will require teachers to relinquish some of their decision-making power and share it with students. It is difficult to convincingly promote music education for its creative and expressive benefits to students if their experiences are solely dominated by the rehearsal of other people's music, under the strict direction of a teacher who prescribes exactly how it should be performed.

This latter approach sounds more like a sports team: a coach creates the game plan, and runs team practice to prepare for the next contest. A similarity with sports can threaten music's place in education. Athletics—not to be confused with its distant cousin, physical education—are squarely part of *extracurricular* activities. It's rare to allot a full-time position in a school for coaching sports. Yet, some music teachers choose to run their classes like coaches run their teams. To be clear, competitive sports can offer many benefits to the young people who participating in them. But few people would say that all children should be on a volleyball team or a wrestling squad. It is reasonable, however, to suggest that all children should have the powerful and life-affirming experience of making music. There are important reasons why sports teams and other enriching clubs happen outside the school curriculum. When music education operates like these groups rather than courses such as math and English, then the whole school music enterprise risks being relegated to extracurricular status. Consequently, music making could become only an option for the few kids with "talent," a frill that is expendable in times of budgetary belt-tightening, or seen as mere entertainment.

In advocating for the inclusion of music in their kids' educational experiences, people need not deny that music is "entertaining" by nature. That position would be downright silly. For many people, music is a top form of entertainment in modern life. People spend many hours of everyday life listening to music. They attend concerts and other musical events with families and friends. And in a favorite of many, people make music together—in community auditoriums, church and temple sanctuaries, park amphitheaters, and also in living rooms, garages, and around the dinner table! These activities can be so important in people's lives. Perhaps, in fighting the perception that music is *just* entertainment, some have missed a larger truth: *entertainment is not just entertainment.*

What is labeled "entertainment" is usually an opportunity to do something enjoyable and emotionally rewarding, and to do it with other people. Even when entertainment seems to be the main purpose of music in a given situation, it is not a throwaway moment or squandered time. Rather it is often a context for people to get in touch with their humanness and to connect with others, which further expands humanness.

Many people are reminded of this every holiday season when they spend time with family and friends. Sure, they exchange gifts and have a few meals together (or many, many meals!). They also enjoy some very rewarding moments together "entertaining" themselves. Some moments are spectator-oriented: watching televised sporting events, seeing a movie, and taking in New Year's Eve music performances on TV. And some of what they do is more participatory: they play cards and board games, go sledding down snowy hillsides, and even participate in the competitive sport of mall shopping. Musically, there is singing and piano and guitar playing, and trumpet-wielding musicians have been known to offer their neighborhood performances of "Auld Lang Syne" when the clock strikes midnight on January 1.

The beginning part of this chapter shared some of the work of musicologist-anthropologist Tom Turino, who makes the important distinction between presentational performance and participatory performance in music. Borrowing from this, it seems reasonable to conclude that musical entertainment serves a greater purpose in people's lives when they are participant music-makers rather than music consumers only. The above holiday examples that include participatory and communal entertaining can truly bring people together. The contexts allows people to form social bonds and affirm their humanness. Music making is most *natural* when it allows for expressive spontaneity—as vernacular musicianship tends to do—and when it is participatory, that is, there is not a rigid distinction between music makers (performers) and the spectators (audience).

Times of entertainment with family and friends are not just throwaway moments in people's lives: they promote feeling connected to others, growing and solidifying relationships, and knowing that we matter to the people in our lives. Even a person's entertainment in solitude—one's alone time listening to music, watching television, or making music for pure enjoyment—also contributes to humanness. These can be critical opportunities for identity development and intrapersonal nurturing. By the music and other entertainment people choose, they can learn about themselves and better establish who they are.

There is an alternative to the sports-team model of music participation for kids in receiving formal music instruction. It involves engaging them in experiences that develop their creativity, such as composing original music. It involves them in collaborating in small groups with peers in which *they* share decisions about how to prepare a piece of music for performance. It involves encouraging and teaching improvisation. This approach doesn't mean abandoning large ensembles, which provide great musical experiences and learning opportunities that cannot be had otherwise. But it may mean forsaking the exclusive dedication of lesson time to teacher-dictated rehearsal.

Many music teachers already teach with this model every day. And many more music teachers who do not teach this way *could*, and *would* if they are encouraged to do so. The profession needs more and more music teachers of this ilk.

So yes, continue to get the word out that music is not merely entertainment. And also do not forget that entertainment itself is not just entertainment, especially when it is participatory.

MAKING MUSIC EDUCATION MORE NATURAL: FROM THE MOUTHS OF MUSIC MAJORS

The research and writings of the best musical minds largely match the personal experiences of music teachers and parents. What is known about the nature of music is informed by much direct input from young people themselves. It is particularly interesting to hear from university music majors as they transition from music student to music teacher and from child to adult. While these students may still have some qualities of childhood, most have acquired adult-level verbal skills required to clearly communicate their musical experiences and aspirations. What they are able to express about the nature of music can be very insightful.

To conclude this chapter, the following ideas for making music learning more natural are illustrated through quotes from sophomore music education majors at the University of Nebraska, responding to the question: What about music is most meaningful and rewarding to you? The insights offered by these young adults are varied and quite revealing. They articulate with passion about their musical loves. Some of their comments, shared with their permission (and names changed), reinforce important points about the nature of music as it relates to kids' learning and development. These translate into guidance to the parents and teachers of music students.

Embrace Learners' Tastes and Treasures

There's no substitute for intrinsic motivation. No adult-generated incentive (or threat) can match the attention and drive produced by intrinsic motivation. Students who are generally "into" what they are doing often have a commitment that will sustain them through many challenges. Their love of certain aspects of a musical activity can spark rapid and long-term growth.

Underclassman college students love to talk about what intrinsically motivates them. Although they are music majors and products of formal music education, they are still regular kids and value opportunities to do more vernacular music. In many formal music education settings, such experience can only be found in show choir, marching band, pep band, musical theatre, and jazz groups. But as with Sophie the Soulful Songstress from earlier in this chapter, many university music majors make time in their lives to play popular songs on guitar or piano. And a few students, even today, report having great fun playing in polka bands!

Perhaps some of students' attraction to popular music activities is due to the overt energy—even physicality—associated with them. young people's engagement and learning may be especially boosted when the activity is, well, active! One student, Katie, said this about performing in show choir:

> I really do not need to be in it for any reason other than the personal joy I get out of rehearsing and performing with this group. I love to dance, and I do not get to do so anywhere else. I also get to sing pop music, something that does not happen often in school music.

Does this kind of experience require abandoning classical music and the repertoire of traditional school concert ensembles? Of course not. These are the perfect vehicles for accomplishing some critical outcomes of music education. But given the facilitating power of intrinsic motivation to learning, a comprehensive music curriculum must be broad and inclusive of multiple musical styles, including those that are familiar to and preferred by students. Some very important learning objectives—improving aural skills, building technical facility, and increasing musical creativity, among many others—can be effectively attained using styles of music that students love.

Make Music a Vehicle for Knowing Others and Oneself

Research is establishing that two broad benefits of music participation are social development and identity formation. Many university music students point to their preferred music activities as means of making friends and stimulating personal growth. Of his favorite musical group, Jared said: "When practicing or performing, I get to be myself. I don't have to put on a 'societal mask' because I'm truly in my element. I am in it purely for the love of the art." Similarly, Aurora said playing her own singer-songwriter material on the piano is "a way to express what I feel on the inside into something more tangible and musical, and help me remember why I love music and why I am working hard at school."

Another student, Melinda, described her experience this way:

> It is important for me to have a group I participate in only out of the pure passion I have to express myself. I also make tons of friends, all whom I consider my family. There is no possible way I could be in this group out of extrinsic motivation because we don't compete, so there are no rewards or grades or gain other than the feeling you get when you are doing what you love, with the people you love.

The social rewards of a music group don't just happen outside of rehearsals and performance. Significant bonding can occur during the music making itself. In Hector's comment below, note that improvisation not only serves a self-expressive purpose, it allows connection to others.

> One very important musical activity for me is free improvisation with friends. It allows me to get away from any written music, and focus solely on the people around me. Free improvisation doesn't mean going crazy on your instrument with no rules. If one person plays an idea, then you're bound to the dynamics, tempo, and roughly the same style of rhythm and articulation. It's similar to someone asking you to paint a rainbow, but they only give you white and black paint. You have certain limits, but you're free to do whatever you need to do in order to reach what you feel is necessary, musically.

Empower Your Young Musicians

Hector's comment above also illustrates how motivating it is to feel autonomy or a sense of control in music. Many of the groups mentioned by university music majors also involve student leadership. Marching bands, for instance, often utilize students as rank leaders or section leaders. It is likely that young musicians are more willing to do hard work when they feel it is *their* work. Another student, Renae, noted the adversities of outdoor rehearsals in Nebraska's sweltering summer heat and bitter winter cold, but concluded, "I miss every second of it in the off season and I crave to go back and work on more drills."

In order for students to feel empowered or invested in an activity, teachers need not relinquish their own leadership role. But they can extend to students more decision-making opportunity. However it is accomplished, student musicians thrive when they feel their contributions are valued and significant. Student Kellen once explained to me that playing a melody instrument provides a "huge feeling of satisfaction and importance." He went on to explain it greater detail:

> It is kind of selfish reasoning, but I just feel important to the group as I play the melody so often, and with an instrument that can be heard by most the audience. I feel like the success of the performance has a great deal to do with me, and I enjoy that responsibility.

Although these students don't typically use the term "intrinsic motivation" when they speak of their music making, they definitely understand the concept. (This is discussed in much more detail in chapter 3, "Motivation for Music.") They have experienced it, and for most of them, it's what has led them to choose music as their major. It is important that they continue to connect with their musical loves as they get deeper into their music education training and throughout their subsequent teaching careers that follow. They may face more and more musical expectations (i.e., extrinsic factors) going forward. But ideally these factors will not stop them from engaging in self-selected music activities. One final student quote, from Wilson, says it well:

> My favorite performance group provides me with an enjoyment that I think all music students should have. Playing in this group is not about making money or even advancing yourself musically, it's about making music for the group.

NOTES

1. Thomas Turino, Music as *Social Life: The Politics of Participation* (Chicago: University of Chicago Press, 2008), 1.

2. Lucy Green, *How Popular Musicians Learn: A Way Ahead for Music Education* (Aldershot, UK: Ashgate, 2002).

3

MOTIVATION FOR MUSIC

Motivation is no simple matter. If mastering motivation was easy, then everyone would be wildly successful in all aspects of their personal and professional lives. And everybody would also have the perfect bodies of the fitness models and professional athletes in the television commercials selling exercise equipment. Incidentally, when it comes to motivation and performance, athletes are very much like musicians.

Unfortunately, one of the ways that performers in these two domains are similar is in the clichés and oversimplifications that are perpetuated about becoming successful. For example, it is often said that victory in an evenly matched sports competition comes down to "who *wants it* more." Similarly, many performers who manage to make it in the music industry credit an "unrelenting pursuit" of their musical dreams.[1] In reality, musical motivation is not one-dimensional, and it certainly is not a matter of simply wanting to be great—even wanting it *really, really badly*.

The motivation of a developing musician is multifaceted and malleable. Even an entire book on the subject—let alone a single chapter like this—is unlikely to allow readers to master motivation. The following pages of this chapter will, however, provide helpful insights around these motivational concepts:

- Contrary to a popular misconception, "intrinsic motivation" does not refer to a drive for success that people feel within themselves. In fact, intrinsic motivation for music is best understood as the

emotional reward that comes from within the act of making music.
- Nurturing one's intrinsic enjoyment of music is critical throughout musical development. A young person who fails to do this is at risk of dropping out as a beginner or burning out as a more experienced musician.
- When kids are motivated to engage in effortful behaviors that are not immediately rewarding but are ultimately valuable, they often rely on others—other people and institutions—for so-called extrinsic motivation.
- Young musicians' motivation can build exponentially as they begin to trust their musicianship such that they fully expect to experience positive results and to accomplish the goals they have for themselves.

A CASE STUDY IN MUSICAL MOTIVATION

During a particularly long and hot American summer years ago, two parents living in a small Southern town had to choose a birthday present for their eleven-year-old son. Since he was a pretty typical boy, the gift ideas were pretty typical. The parents had their options narrowed to a bicycle or a guitar. While not the only factor in the decision, there was a considerable price difference between the two. The more expensive bike was passed over, and the boy received his first guitar on his birthday.

A musical instrument seemed the perfect gift for a boy who had shown great fondness for music all of his childhood. He sang every chance he got, especially in and around church, but he also found opportunities at family gatherings, at school, and while playing in the backyard with friends. He was probably the kind of kid who sang about every spoonful of cereal at breakfast. People enjoyed his singing and he constantly fielded song requests from teachers and friends. He eventually entered a talent show at the local fairgrounds, where he won second prize. His parents figured the gift of a guitar made sense as it would help him further develop his singing. After the boy received some tutoring from a couple of his uncles who played, and armed with a few chords and recordings of his favorite music, he labored to reproduce the sounds he loved. His singing likely benefited from this practice but not enough to keep pace with the increase in musical expectations that come when a singing child becomes a singing teenager. His eighth-grade music teacher saw no special potential in him and did not invite him to perform in the school's top vocal group. He began to identify the musical settings in which his skills were best suited. He jumped at certain performance opportunities—he especially enjoyed making music for and with his friends—and avoided other performance settings with equal enthusiasm.

His love for music was never shaken and his involvement in it never stopped. In high school he participated in sports and other school clubs, but he often willingly sacrificed leisure activities in order to do music. Because his family struggled financially, he also took part-time jobs. As a teen he worked at a downtown theater, then later at a metal products factory. Upon graduating from high school he took a full-time job driving a delivery truck for a tool factory. But music remained his passion. He kept at it despite adversity: at an unsuccessful audition for a local vocal quartet, he was told that he couldn't sing.

On many of his deliveries, this singing guitar-playing truck driver passed a small recording studio. It offered a make-your-own-recording service to anybody willing to pay the studio costs. The young man's first recorded song impressed the studio's office manager, who then shared a copy with the record producer who owned the studio. With only moderate interest, the producer waited nearly a year before approaching the aspiring singer. Under the tutelage of the producer, the young musician still struggled, but the producer eventually matched him up with some more experienced musicians in hopes of developing his skills. What followed were many more months of hard work.

But by now, young Elvis Presley was fully committed to a musical life.

It deserves mention that once Elvis did get his "big break" and performed for the first time at the Grand Ole Opry radio program in Nashville, he was no instant success. In fact, the head of the Opry talent office, after hearing Elvis's performance, told him that he should go back to driving a truck!

Although certain parts of Elvis's biography are very unusual—especially after achieving stardom—some aspects of his development are common to many musicians: a love of music, the support of others, maximizing available resources, and persevering through adversity. As described above, it was a combination of environmental factors and experiences that allowed a young boy from Tupelo, Mississippi, by way of Memphis, to become "The King."

Well, to be more precise, a number of factors allowed him to develop a real musicianship that, combined with other personal qualities, helped him to succeed in the music business. While Elvis's uniqueness as a performer and his celebrity may lead regular people to see him as extraordinary, his musicianship is definitely accessible to others. Most rock scholars agree that from a strictly musical standpoint, Elvis was not a spectacular talent. He developed his musical skills much like everybody else does.

A lot can be learned from Elvis's motivation. He formed a deep connection to music, likely because his earliest exposures to it were in enjoyable social contexts in which the emotional aspects of the experience were paramount. As a youngster he had the freedom to initiate the kinds of musical activities that appealed to him, and the people around him supported him and gave him positive attention for his music making. He believed that music was *his* thing, as opposed to something that others expected him to do. This belief likely contributed much to his seeking out new opportunities, including in school, and his desire to broaden his musical horizons.

Perhaps the greatest insight is that Elvis sustained his interest in music despite distraction and hardship. Occasional failures did not cause him to abandon his quest to be a musician. The best explanation for this is that even as a youth Elvis had built a strong and positive sense of musical *self-efficacy*. Psychologists define self-efficacy as a person's judgments about his or her ability to plan and carry out the actions needed to accomplish a specific performance task. More simply put, self-efficacy refers to people's *trust* in their own ability. Musicians with high self-efficacy expect to do well in their performance endeavors, and when they have a less-than-successful performance, they see it as a learning experience rather than a reason to quit. It's easy to imagine young Elvis Presley having this mindset. Throughout his ups and downs, he seemed to always believe in his musical abilities, that they were good enough to accomplish what he wanted, and that he was always improving them.

INTRINSIC MOTIVATION FOR MUSIC LEARNING

The more researchers study motivation, the more complex and fascinating it is revealed to be. People often talk about motivation as if it's merely a feeling that overcomes them. They may skip their plan to go the gym to work out because they're "just not motivated right now." Musicians often complain of not being motivated to practice. Of course, what they're really saying is they just don't *feel like* practicing. Some musicians seem content to wait (and wait . . . and wait . . .) to start a practice session until they do *feel like it*. Many so-called motivational speakers exploit this mindset and simply try to stir up the feelings of their listeners. Those in the audience may make ambitious plans during the inspiring speech, but ultimately ignore them afterward when the feelings have faded and the speaker has traveled on to the next presentation (with paycheck in hand).

Motivation is certainly linked to the beliefs we hold and the emotions we experience but, to quote the old Boston song, it really is "more than a feeling." Many people are so attracted to music as children that they want to learn a musical instrument. Yet relatively few of them ever learn to play one well. Why? Because it entails a great deal of effort! The kind of practicing that is required is not enjoyable. Even the most highly successful musicians admit that they do not like to practice. So why do they end up doing it anyway?

While practice per se is rarely pleasurable, many experiences within music are. Growing musically requires a combination of intrinsic and extrinsic motivation. An activity that is intrinsically motivating is one that is rewarding *in itself* (perhaps like eating junk food). The activity is its own reward. In contrast, an activity that is extrinsically motivated is done for a reason outside of the activity (perhaps like eating a vegetable salad with no dressing). People do it because they expect positive consequences from doing it.

Understanding the meaning of intrinsic and extrinsic motivation is important. A very common misconception is that intrinsic motivation is a desire that comes from within a person. Yes, intrinsic motivation does come from *within*, but it comes from within *the activity* itself, *not* from within the person. This is important because some very powerful drives that people feel within themselves are, in fact, extrinsically motivated. For example, many people feel driven to succeed in their chosen professions. They might feel it so strongly and from so deeply within their core that it seems like an innate drive or even a compulsion. It is powerful motivation to be sure, but not intrinsic. Instead, there can be the expectation of a positive outcome, such as the goals of highly competitive driven athletes, for example to win a championship, or earn a new high-dollar contract. In contrast, athletes who are truly intrinsically motivated play their sport simply, as it were, "for the love of the game." So too a young musician who is driven to be the best may not be acting on intrinsic motivation when engaged in their music making.

Why belabor this point? Is the distinction between intrinsic and extrinsic motivation that important? Just because young people sing along to their favorite recordings because they enjoy it (intrinsic), and they practice scales because it builds their performance facility (extrinsic) . . . what good comes from knowing this?

Consider the cautionary value of understanding this: a person whose musical life is devoid of intrinsic motivation is at risk of dropping out as a beginner or burning out as a more experienced musician. Young people who find their musical involvement dominated by extrinsically motivated activities are in danger of quitting music altogether. Some college music majors have been heard to say as seniors, "I can't wait until my final recital is done, so I'll never have to perform again." It is sad that performance—presumably the act of sharing music with people who want to hear it—has become something that some musicians feel they "have to" do.

True intrinsic motivation can be incredibly effective in moving young musicians forward in their growth and skill development. It can explain why many past rock and jazz musicians became proficient performers, all without any formal instruction. It is common for these so-called vernacular musicians to have spent their childhoods in rich musical environments, such as trumpet great Louis Armstrong growing up in the jazz culture of New Orleans. Children with vernacular music upbringings do not receive private lessons (in any formal sense) or depend on school music experiences. They do, however, experience their natural love of music being nurtured by hearing great music all around them and through enjoyable music-making experiences with peers and more advanced performers. They learn the music that surrounds them—in their *real lives* the stuff that is familiar to them, the stuff they love. They have such personal, emotional, and social connections to the kind of music they are making that they are willing to invest time doing it and getting better at it.

Vernacular musicians benefit greatly from the nurturing of their intrinsic motivation; however, the takeaway is not that formal music education can be abandoned altogether. Rather, teachers and parents can draw on the concept of vernacular musicianship to promote intrinsic motivation in their music students.

Intrinsic motivation is fostered when people have *choice and personal autonomy* in their activities. Motivated musicians are able to "take ownership," as the catchphrase goes. Research suggests that musicians willingly invest more time and attention on material that they have chosen for themselves.[2] Feeling empowered and having a sense of self-determination are characteristics that distinguish play from work. So when young people feel like they have choice and freedom in their music learning, devoting time and energy can seem much less onerous and effortful.

Musicians-in-training also benefit greatly if their studies *include their musical loves*. As alluded to earlier, many young people choose to study music because they love music. Usually what attracts them to music is its ability to express emotions and produce powerful feelings in people. There may be a particular style of music that they would listen to for hours at a time any chance they get. But all too often, formally trained music students find themselves focusing mostly on technical performance issues (over expressive ones), and working on music that is nothing like what is on their music app's playlists. Music learning can be enhanced when students' assignments and practice connect to what they really love about music.

Motivation for music learning can also be bolstered greatly when it *emphasizes the social aspects of music making*. Human beings are social creatures. We are driven to connect with each other in a variety of ways. For many people, this is the reason they get involved with music. Lots of teenagers choose to join the high-school music program—or drop out of it—in order to be with their friends. But the social dynamic of a musical life is not just goofy teenagers collapsing under peer pressure. The social is a natural part of music making all around the world. On the other hand, in formal education, there are plenty of times when young musicians must do solitary practicing and when they are in ensemble classes with the expectation of "no talking during rehearsal."

Those times are necessary and valuable, but sustaining kids through them is accomplished through other experiences building social bonds with their fellow musicians. This can occur before and after rehearsals and during travel time to performance events, but it can also happen during rehearsals and performances if music students are allowed to productively interact with each other. Connecting with others through artistic expression is a powerful reward.

WHEN DESIRE IS FOUND WANTING

Some people can work a job they hate for years, and even make a career of it. It is, however, very rare for someone in the arts to last long without some measure of love for the subject matter. Many professional musicians can recall a "love at first sight" or "love at first sound" experience during childhood which started a lifelong infatuation with music. As young people develop their performance skills, there's no substitute for their own enjoyment and interest in music. In many ways, intrinsic motivation—the simple desire to do something for its own sake—is the most important ingredient in long-term musical success.

Of course not all aspects of music performance are pleasant. Musicians can find themselves competing for positions, gigs, and other performance opportunities (e.g., recording contracts). Though success in these ventures can be exhilarating, the failures can take a psychological toll. Also, some performance activities involve heavy doses of criticism and being judged by others. The stressful aspects of a musician's life can chip away at a simple love of the art and the desire to lead a musical life. Young musicians may even question whether they want to do music at all, thinking, "I didn't know that something so fun could end up being so hard."

Such conditions can put pressure on young musicians to improve their skills as much and as quickly as possible. And nothing can be more disenchanting to a music-loving performer than the demands of practice. When it comes to "what works" for skill improvement, there's a certain kind of practice that psychologists have identified as the key contributor to growth in performance skills. This *deliberate practice* is defined as being (1) effortful and concentration-heavy, (2) done in isolation, and (3) focused on deficiencies in performance.[3] As such, practicing really cannot be intrinsically motivating to many people: it's hard, it's lonely, and forces you to think about your shortcomings! But deliberate practice enables musicians to most efficiently build their skills.

That said, practice need not always be unpleasant to be effective. The musicians' attitude heading into practice sessions can make a big difference. If they dwell on the effort involved and the wish to be doing something else, then their practice may be very tough sledding. But with an identified goal of learning something new, they will likely exit the session having improved and feeling glad that they put in the time. In terms of enjoyment, however, practice really cannot compete with other musical activities such as jamming with friends or taking part in a group production for an enthusiastic audience. But not only does deliberate practice foster greater musical growth, it also allows enjoyment of the rewards of these other activities.

Especially for young musicians, practice is almost always extrinsically motivated. It is not done for the sake of it, but for the promising outcomes from having done it. Musical children gain much from the encouragement of parents and teachers. And young people who persist in music—whether in school ensembles or garage bands—often do so because of peer support. Then, too, what musician is not driven to practice by an impending performance? The extrinsic rewards of music involvement can make the necessity of practice more palatable to aspiring performers.

Extrinsic motivators can be so present and effective that musicians automatically begin to internalize them. Prominent motivation researchers Edward Deci and Richard Ryan have advanced a Self-Determination Theory, which can be used to explain how musicians come to accept the hard work of practice.[4] They describe extrinsic motivation as having four levels, progressing from external to internal. Here's how the theory applies to musicians and practice:

1. "I *have to* practice." *External regulation*, as the researchers call it, shows compliance; the activity is done purely to obtain rewards and avoid punishments.
2. "I *ought to* practice." *Introjected regulation*, so called, shows self-control; doing the activity produces feelings of pride and helps avoid feelings of guilt.

3. "I *need to* practice." *Identified regulation* shows valuing of the activity; it is done because the benefits are experienced as real, so the activity has become personally important.
4. "I practice." *Integrated regulation* shows adoption; the activity is done because it is has been assimilated into one's identity.

Note that even when extrinsic motivation has been fully internalized (integrated regulation), this does not make it intrinsic. It does not result in musicians thinking "I *want* to practice." It does, however, have them practicing as a regular part of life. They likely no longer wonder if they should practice, or how to find time to do it. With apologies to Nike, they just do it.

Below, a great quote from concert pianist André Watts shows his progression through the levels of extrinsic motivation to practice (with research terminology added in parentheses):

> I wouldn't be a pianist today if my mother hadn't made me practice (external). . . . On days when I wasn't exactly moved to practice, my mother saw to it that I did. Sometimes she tried coaxing me to the piano by relating the careers of famous musicians, hoping perhaps to inspire me to practice (introjected). At thirteen, however, I realized the necessity of practice (identified). I still don't really "like" it all the time, but by now it has become second nature (integrated).[5]

Watts' term "second nature" is an apt description of his practicing. Second nature refers to a behavior that has become so routine that it seems instinctive. There are many music-making behaviors that are "first nature"—meaning, they're inherently gratifying—but practicing isn't one of them.

Another fantastic musician, Grammy Award–winning bassist and singer Esperanza Spalding, once described her approach to practice as an "everyday, diligent, warrior-like mentality." Rather than seeing practicing as a necessary evil or a burden, she said of her approach, "I really like that. It's liberating somehow."[6] What she likely means is that she feels freed from any deliberation about whether or not to practice. She just does it.

Anyone who has seen André Watts or Esperanza Spalding perform can tell that they love music. That underlying love sustained them through the rigors of training and demanding performance schedules.

But they also accepted the hard work of musicianship. Balance is key. People cannot be practice robots that pound away at only the most challenging skill-building études. On the other hand, aspiring musicians will not go far if they do only what is musically fun.

Performers should seek to experience the rewards that practice brings, knowing that greater skill empowers them. Improved skill decreases focus on producing their own performance, and frees them to explore new artistic possibilities and interact more deeply with coperformers. As they experience these benefits, practice can become a less onerous and a more automatic part of life—and one that can provide considerable payoff in the end.

LEARNING TO LOVE PRACTICE . . . AND OTHER (VIRTUALLY) IMPOSSIBLE FEATS

Some young people grow up to devote their lives to musical pursuits, while others who were similarly talented as kids give up music as adults. After people have matured beyond the playful days of early childhood, having satisfying music-making experiences requires more than a childlike spirit of creativity and enthusiasm for exploring musical sound. In order to make music that matches their ideals (i.e., what sounds good to them), people need to possess a level of skill that doesn't come easily. It takes a certain level of dedication and effort to develop that skill. Some do what it takes and others do not. Even among the ones that do it, rarely do musicians come to think favorably about the act of practicing.

Must it be this way? Can practicing be an activity that musicians enjoy? You may know musicians who seem to like practicing, and report they always love singing or playing their instrument. This may be true, but perhaps most musicians who claim they enjoy practicing may have a very loose definition of practice. They may not realize that they are actually doing it wrong! Solitude and concentration applied in practice are key ingredients for musicians to develop their skills. Practicing is made more productive if it is entered into with *specific goals in mind*, and carried out with an *ear toward error detection and correction*. In other words, true practice requires additional prep time (for goal setting) and constant mental focus during the activity. It is far easier to go into a session without much forethought and to "practice" whatever appeals in the moment. It's far easier but not likely to produce growth and new skills. But the effort of quality practicing pays off.

Although it is surely uncommon, some musicians manage to experience enjoyment in deliberate practice. Several conditions foster this outcome. Musicians must have strong confidence in the process of practice: they are certain that it works. Furthermore, not only do they know results will come, they believe that they will experience (feel or hear) the results for themselves, and it will happen sooner rather than later. Their practicing is efficient, characterized by conscious goal setting and self-monitoring as mentioned above. Perhaps in the best-case scenario, musicians become so engaged that they become fascinated with the phenomenon of practice itself. It becomes a time to experiment with new strategies and test theories about oneself. Perhaps you know people who seem to approach their overall personal betterment with this mindset. Musicians who do this with their practicing can come to think of themselves as private investigators of the performance process or musical explorers. Beyond just capturing a great performance at the end of the process, practicing is about the "thrill of the hunt."

For those who are not investigators in the practice room, reasons for practicing are typically more pragmatic. Most musicians practice because of an upcoming performance. Even the most advanced musicians and accomplished performers practice because there's a concert or gig coming up and they want it to go well. Practicing amounts to delayed gratification. The effort required to practice pays off when they experience the reward of a successful performance.

Ideally, the desired payoffs of practice are musical in nature. That is, musicians define a "successful" performance by their experiencing the emotional rewards of music making, which is qualitatively different from defining success as simply avoiding embarrassment in performance. Improvements in skill allow developing musicians to engage in more gratifying performance experiences and to enjoy the powerful aesthetic enrichment that accompanies music making. This is why intrinsic motivation is so important. Intrinsically motivating experiences must be a part of a musical life in order for it to survive. If young musicians' practice leads only to musical performances that they don't enjoy—or even dread, as is the case with performance anxiety—they are likely heading for burnout. Because of this, informal music making can make a great supplement or even alternative to formal public performances. Whether an impromptu sing-a-long at a social gathering, a jam session in the garage with friends, or a "family room concert series," such experiences can reconnect people to the most human rewards of music.

ENCOURAGING GREATER MOTIVATION IN MUSIC STUDENTS

Teachers and parents of musical kids want the best for them. These adults are willing to invest their own time and energy to support their students in their musical efforts. Of course, it is no use to try to force them to do what is good for them (like practice) with a simple promise of "You'll thank me later for making you do it." This final section incorporates the major points about motivation discussed earlier in this chapter and offers specific guidelines on how adults can foster in young people the motivation that leads to musical achievement.

Personalize and Diversify Motivational Strategies

Any educational expert selling a "one size fits all" approach to human learning is surely a better salesperson than educator! *What works* for motivating people can differ dramatically from one person to another. Successfully applying the motivational principles and ideas offered in this chapter (and book) require teachers and parents to *really know* their music students. Adults can help personalize their young musicians' motivation by letting them make music *their* "thing" *however they do this*. A young person's musical involvement needs to evolve in its own natural, unique way. Children may end up having musical experiences that differ dramatically from those of their parents and teachers. Whereas a particular parent or teacher may have loved being in the high-school band, perhaps their young musician finds a musical home base in the school choir—or perhaps in a music setting outside school altogether.

Similarly, when it comes to choosing strategies to motivate kids, adults can mistakenly consider only their ideas of what *should* motivate young people. By way of illustration, experienced teachers know that the threat of a bad grade is no fool-proof strategy to motivate students to pay attention in class or to do their homework; some students *in reality* do not care about grades even though they probably *should*. An incentive that will work with a young musician will be one that is personally meaningful to that individual. Knowing what is actually "meaningful" to a person requires knowing that person very well.

In fact, the above example of threats of a bad grade is a poor motivational approach even for grade-conscious kids. This is because *threatening (anything) is never a good strategy in music learning*. Anxiety impedes learning. Fear is part of the very definition of anxiety. This is not advice to shield young people from real-life negative consequences from a lack of applying themselves. But experiencing negative consequences after the fact is quite different than trying to scare a young musician before the fact. Even a meaningful threat depends on generating fear within the music learner. Motivation to avoid a poor performance is *not* the same as motivation to give a good performance. There are serious long-term consequences of linking fear to music performance and developing a mentality of avoiding bad outcomes. These are killers of intrinsic motivation for music, and as such can contribute greatly to dropout and burnout.

Find Fulfilling Performances to Practice For

In deterring young musicians from developing an avoidance mentality, help them find performances to practice *for*. Organized and mindful practice is essential for music students to reach their performance skill potential. Most, however, will not do this kind of effortful practicing with only the abstract goal of becoming a better musician. It can be better to have the more tangible goal of an upcoming performance. And to reinforce the above warning about anxiety, the value of having a performance to practice *for* is valid without it being a "special" public performance before a large or intimidating audience. If concerts and recitals in formal settings are perceived as "high stakes," then young musicians may be able to rediscover within more informal settings their intrinsic motivation for music making.

Internalize Extrinsic Sources of Motivation

Ideally, as young musicians develop, they begin to internalize the extrinsic sources of motivation that were previously provided by important others in their lives (i.e., parents, teachers, and peers). With beginners, it is usually necessary for parents to offer meaningful rewards for their children practicing, be they extra treats for dessert or the preservation of electronics screen-time privileges. Similarly, teachers play a critical role by offering constructive verbal feedback to encourage young learners. If done properly, though, as young musicians mature, they take on for themselves the values shown to them by these important others. Instead of relying on parents, they start to believe that they "treat" themselves by doing the work that yields musically enriching skill improvement. They can replace the praise of a respected teacher with a self-supplied positive message: *I did this activity because it was important to me and I enjoy the benefits.*

Teachers and parents have many options for supporting young musicians' advancement on the continuum of internalizing extrinsic motivation. Adults can talk to their kids about this development process and commend them when they show instances of growth (perhaps something like "You only had to practice twenty minutes to earn the reward I offered, but I noticed you practiced a full thirty minutes anyway, and it sure paid off. That song sounds great!"). Young musicians also need opportunities to be around peer musicians, including those who are more advanced, whose more mature musical value systems can rub off on them.

Build Musical Self-Efficacy

As music students practice and engage in the music making activities that allow them to improve their skills, we must bring this to their attention and celebrate the improvement. Their own skill development is not always readily apparent to them because the growth often comes so gradually that they do not recognize the change. Teachers and parents can point out times when they remember their young musicians *not being able* to do something that they *can now do*. Praise should be offered not just for the improvement made, but especially for the time and energy they invested to make it happen.

Adults can also support their musical kids by talking with them about their practicing process. With listening and without preaching, bring attention to organizing practice sessions around goals and to identifying performance problems in order to try out new strategies to fix them. As they are developmentally able, engage young musicians in "bigger picture" evaluation of their own practicing approaches. Perhaps they'll take to the role of being a musical detective, looking for clues (to musical breakthroughs) and testing out theories about what makes their practicing more efficient and productive. Remember to have dialogue.

As musicians increase confidence in their own practicing and skill advancement, they increase confidence in themselves as musicians. They are building real and practical trust in their own musicianship. And there is perhaps nothing more motivating to people than trusting themselves such that they fully expect to experience positive results and to accomplish the goals they have for themselves.

NOTES

1. Michael Ramirez, *Destined for Greatness: Passion, Dreams, and Aspirations in a College Music Town* (New Brunswick, NJ: Rutgers University Press, 2018).

2. Gary E. McPherson, Jane W. Davidson, and Robert Faulkner, "Chapter 2: Initial Music Learning and Practice," in *Music in Our Lives: Rethinking Musical Ability, Development and Identity* (Oxford: Oxford University Press, 2012), 19–43. In a section titled "Learner Autonomy and Choice in Practice," the authors review research that clearly indicates that when students are allowed to choose materials used in their studies, they can experience significant increases in intrinisic motivation and task engagement. In one case study they review, a beginning clarinetist practiced a piece she chose for herself *ten times* as much as she practiced the piece she was assigned by her teacher!

3. K. Anders Ericsson and Andreas C. Lehmann, "Expertise," in *Encyclopedia of Creativity, Vol. 1*, edited by Mark A. Runco and Steven R. Pritzker, 488–96 (New York: Academic Press, 2011).

4. Richard M. and Edward L. Deci, "Self-Determination Theory and the Facilitation of Intrinsic Motivation, Social Development, and Well-Being," *American Psychologist* 55, no. 1 (2000): 68–78.

5. Elyse Mac, *Great Pianists Speak for Themselves* (New York: Dodd, Mead and Company, 1980), 182.

6. Abigail Pesta, "All That Jazz," *Newsweek* 159, no. 8 (February 20, 2012): 53–54.

4

CREATIVITY IN MUSIC

Many people are fascinated by artists, musicians, writers, and inventors, whose lives seem occupied by creativity. Most of the general public seems content to be consumers and audience members who enjoy the creative output of others, without attempting to be creative themselves. They may look at artists and innovators with admiration, and wonder, "How do they think this stuff up?"

Similarly, formal study of music is sometimes credited with developing young peoples' creative thinking skills. On the surface at least, this seems quite reasonable given that music is an art, and human's primary purpose for the arts is usually understood to be creative expression. Upon deeper consideration, however, we must concede that simply learning to play a musical instrument or becoming a fine singer does not necessarily lead musicians to become more artistically creative.

This chapter provides helpful insights into creativity, including these broad takeaway points:

- Creative artists do not aspire to merely become experts in their field. Rather, they are inclined to explore it to discover new ways of doing things.
- Although some may believe that being a perfectionist leads to greatness, in reality, a perfectionistic mentality can be a major hindrance to developing creativity.
- A boost in musical creativity does not just benefit those who want to be composers or songwriters. A more creative musicianship can

also deepen the perspective that young musicians bring to their performing activities.

CREATIVE ARTISTS: A DIFFERENT BREED OR A DIFFERENT CREED?

Perhaps because of the observer's effect, many people have concluded that creative individuals are fundamentally different from everyone else. That is, they have a different makeup. They are endowed with an uncommon gift, or their brains are wired in a special way. Creative artists are simply a different breed.

There is, however, an alternative explanation. Creative individuals are unique primarily in their values, goals, and approach to life. Their brains may indeed be different, but perhaps they've become that way. Creative people may develop differently as a result of going through their lives with different motivations and from understanding their experiences with a different perspective.

The Endgame: Expertise or Exploration?

One of the hallmarks of creativity can be seen in artists' motivations. After becoming involved in a certain field—say, music, painting, or poetry—some people proceed with the goal of being the best they can be, to be a highly skilled musician, painter, or poet. But creative artists approach their activities a bit differently. Their orientation is not merely toward becoming an expert in their chosen field. They are motivated to more fully explore the field or even challenge it.

Many young people fall in love with music and want to become career musicians. Such a person may envision the kind of musician he or she wants to be, try to learn the requisite skills, and seek opportunities that lead to that destination goal. In contrast, those who are traditionally considered "creative" may travel on a different, more exploratory path. As they gain musical expertise, they also pursue the larger goals of realizing original ideas and experimenting with new ways of doing music.

Psychologist Howard Gardner has considered the minds of artists and great thinkers for decades. Much of his work has involved in-depth study of the lives of extraordinary people like Virginia Woolf, Pablo Picasso, Igor Stravinsky, and Albert Einstein. He has cited Mozart and Beethoven as an example of an expert and a creative individual, respectively:

> Mozart is the master. Mozart, in my view, wrote the most beautiful music ever. But Mozart was not somebody who was trying to create a new domain. He was not interested in creating new genres. He wrote in the genres of his time, and just did it so beautifully that he forced, in a sense, his successors to become Beethoven, to be Romantics, to overthrow classical music, because nobody could do it as well as Mozart.[1]

Although readers may not accept his appraisal of these great composers, the quote describes the difference between a domain acceptor and a domain challenger. Obviously, both kinds of artists are important. Perhaps, as Gardner suggests, they even depend on each other.

Failure: To Be Avoided or to Be Exploited?

A more specific component of the creative mindset centers on beliefs about failure. Nobody enjoys failing at something that they care about, especially if that something is used to define one's identity. But creative people may take a bigger-picture perspective. Not being able to do something (i.e., failure) is a kind of prerequisite to learning and improvement. Creative artists accept failure as merely part of the process, whereas others may see it as a reason to quit.

The next chapter on improvisation considers how suspending self-consciousness is key in creative thought and performance. "Self-consciousness" can be a misleading term. Often one's inner critic simply voices fears about what other people might say. Self-consciousness can really reflect concern about other's opinions. Could it be that creative artists just have less regard for the criticism of others? They may not be less sensitive (to criticism) than most people, but proportional to their preoccupation with their art, they are less *influenced* by criticism.

To creative artists, the praise of critics and applause of audiences are not the primary means of defining success. Feedback from others is a source of information, or an opportunity to better understand how their work affects people. A poorly received performance or product—a "flop," a "bust," or even an "epic fail"—is embraced as a lesson learned. In this way, creative artists may ultimately come to define failure differently than others do. They are not primarily worried about failing to impress an audience. Rather, failure equals not being fully engaged in your art. The amazing cellist Yo-Yo Ma once described a moment of revelation he had:

> While sitting there at the concert, playing all the notes correctly, I started to wonder, "Why am I here? I'm doing everything as planned. So what's at stake? Nothing. Not only is the audience bored but I myself am bored." Perfection is not very communicative. However, when you subordinate your technique to the musical message you get really involved. Then you can take risks. It doesn't matter if you fail.[2]

Of course, it's easy for Yo-Yo Ma to say this . . . he *actually is* playing all the notes correctly! But it applies to us nonvirtuosi as well.

People We Admire: Role Models or Inspirers?

As explained throughout this book, there are plenty of reasons to put less stock in the "nature" explanation of musicianship and more in the "nurture." The same goes for the development of creativity. Everyone has the capacity to be highly creative. With the right opportunities and experiences, virtually anyone can develop the mindset of a creative artist.

Obviously though, this doesn't happen with many people in our society. Even among talented musicians and artists, many do not adopt a creative mindset. Could a potential hindrance be the use of role models? By definition, a role model is someone who is an example to be emulated. While imitation is a natural and effective way to learn many skills, primarily aspiring to "be like" or "as good as" an admired artist may not be conducive to the creative spirit. The desire to be "good enough" or "make it" as a musician could override a creative drive to advance one's understanding and fully engage in the art.

It may be more constructive for young people to look to admired artists for inspiration: inspiration to develop their own creativity. In fact, as Howard Gardner did in considering the lives of great minds, perhaps we can all learn from identifying creative artists' creed, the set of values that guide their activities. There's inspiration to be had whether we aspire to innovate the field in which we work, or more simply wish to better express ourselves through our art.

THE ARTIST'S BATTLE WITHIN

Artistry and expertise are domain specific. This means that someone who is particularly creative as a musician will not necessarily be creative as a writer or a painter or a chef. But there are major commonalities in the creative process across all disciplines. Music composers and creative writers can sound very similar when they talk about the challenges faced and the rewards gained in their endeavors. There appears be a kind of creative mindset that is needed to be successful, regardless of whether the medium is music, words, paint, or food.

Much music making around us is reproductive rather than creative. Formal groups from professional orchestras to school choirs perform the published works of composers. Aspiring rock bands play "cover" versions of others' songs, and even the most popular artists can feel obligated to offer in live performances exact replicas of what they recorded in the studio. As much as audiences enjoy hearing the familiar, there are some insights into music that can only be gained by creating original material for oneself. Unfortunately, immersion into reproductive music performance can make composing or improvising new music a scary prospect. But a disinclination to creativity is not natural. On the contrary, young children are natural creators, be it through singing spontaneous songs, drawing personally expressive pictures, or thinking up imaginative stories. To paraphrase Picasso, the problem is remaining creative when we're grown up.

The parallels between creative writing and creative music making can be striking. People who have tried to do both often find common struggles in the two domains, including the phenomenon known as "writers' block." This phenomenon seems quite common. It involves staring at the blank page (whether literally or figuratively) with no ideas flowing. Instead of tapping into deep emotions to drive creative expression, a blocked writer/composer can experience debilitating feelings of self-doubt, disinterest, or just a desire to do something else entirely!

It seems that many artists successfully overcome these experiences of blocked creativity by separating from themselves. That is, they see the creation of original material as coming from somewhere other than themselves. Some have conceived of it as being visited by a muse or an angel. Or they may simply accept the ideas that are "out there" and providing them an artist portal through which they can enter reality.

One person who has taken a particular interest in overcoming writer's block is *Eat, Pray, Love* author Elizabeth Gilbert, who once gained valuable insight in an interview she did with singer-songwriter Tom Waits. She recounted Waits's philosophy that each song is its own entity and must be dealt with uniquely. She described his message this way:

> Every song has a distinctive identity that it comes into the world with. It needs to be taken in different ways. He said there are songs that you have to sneak up on like you're hunting for a rare bird. And there are songs that come fully intact like a dream taken through a straw. And there are songs that you find little bits of like pieces of gum underneath the desk. And you scrape them off and you put them together and you make something out of it. And there are songs, he said, that need to be bullied. He said he's been in the studio working on a song and the whole album is done and this one song won't give itself over. And he said everyone's gotten used to seeing him do things like this, he'll march up and down the studio talking to the song saying, "The rest of the family is in the car, we're all going on vacation! You coming along or not? You got ten minutes or else you're getting left behind!" He's like, "You've got to shake it down sometimes."

Gilbert went on to explain that hearing Waits describe it this way resulted in a shift in her own "center of gravity" because it was the first time she thought of creative inspiration as a "thing" she could talk to![3]

Unlike Waits and Gilbert, other creative artists look inward. They believe the ideas come from within, and that their job is to allow that part of themselves to speak. In her book *The Right to Write*, Julia Cameron describes her solution to writer's block as thinking of writing as *taking* dictation, not giving it. "Once writing becomes an act of listening instead of an act of speech, a great deal of the ego goes out of it. . . . We retire as the self-conscious author and become something else: the vehicle for self-expression. When we are just the vehicle, we often write very well. We certainly write more easily."[4] This sentiment is echoed by author Oliver Sacks, who wrote among other books the wonderful and provocative *Musicophilia*. He described one of those breakthrough moments as feeling inside himself "a wonderful associative engine which weaves thoughts togethers and brings unexpected things into apposition." Rather than feeling like he was doing it, he experienced it as though the engine was pulling ideas out of him. "I felt the book was being dictated to me." He added, "I was passive. I was the bridge. I was the transmitter."[5]

Whether conceived of as coming from within or without, interfacing with that expressive source is a key to creativity. It requires us to suspend our own critical voice. In his series of *Inner Game* books, author Timothy Gallwey describes all performers as having both a Self 1 that's controlling and judgmental, and a Self 2 that's free and naturally expressive. (Gallwey's ideas are anecdotal to be sure, but many line up well with what the research says about managing performance anxiety.)[6] Sometimes that critical voice is plainly negative and floods our minds with self-doubt and defeatist thinking. Other times we more subtly sabotage ourselves with the mindset of perfectionism. We may argue that perfectionism is an asset that ultimately ensures our work will be of the highest quality. But more frequently, a perfectionist mentality prevents artists from having the freedom to be creative at all.

Among those who write about writing, one of the most beloved is Anne Lamott. In her fantastic book *Bird by Bird* she offers advice to struggling authors who cannot let their thoughts flow into a first draft because they are too concerned that the initial wording doesn't sound like a polished final product. "Perfectionism is the voice of the oppressor," she says. She gives great encouragement toward quieting the inner critic to allow more free personal expression. She also calls perfectionism a "mean, frozen form of idealism" but "messes are the artist's true friend."[7]

The hard and messy work of creativity can be especially difficult for musicians whose training and performance activities have been dominated by other people's music. They may need to learn a new kind of mental discipline in order to silence the self-critical voice. But even experienced composers—and writers and painters and chefs—struggle with the creative process. Many are constantly devising new strategies to disable that judgmental force within and strengthening their resolve to battle against it. Author Steven Pressfield gives great insight into this in his book *The War of Art*, which is subtitled *Break through the Blocks and Win Your Inner Creative Battles*.[8] It seems that most artists believe that creativity involves both inspiration and perspiration, though there's less agreement about how much of each is required, and from where the inspiration comes. For her part, Elizabeth Gilbert offers: "I think the angels reward people who are at their desk at six o'clock in the morning working."[9]

A GLIMPSE INTO A GROUP CREATIVE PROCESS

In terms of social dynamics, it is impressive to watch a group of musicians, who are strangers to each other, take the stage together for the very first time and make music immediately. I suppose this kind of thing is not exclusive to music though. In sports, there's the pick-up basketball game that commonly takes place in public parks and gyms. The corporate world has ad hoc committees and the justice system throws together a "jury of your peers" for criminal trials. These "zero-history groups" are interesting for exploring how people get along (or not) with each other.

Some musicians are so good that they can all show up for a gig and without knowing each other, and without any rehearsal, they can put on a quality performance that the audience loves. This is pretty common in the jazz world. Groups like this are able to perform on the spot because they all share a common knowledge base. If, say, four jazz musicians are hired and they've never played together, they would talk before and during the gig to figure out the songs that they all know. Plus they would rely on standard conventions of jazz performance along the way.

But what about a group of musicians who come together for the first time to create a completely new piece of music to be recorded? We're not just talking about strangers functioning together and carrying out the things that each of them already knows how to do. Now we're talking about group creativity. Here's where it really gets interesting!

Singer-songwriter-guitarist John Mayer has taken part in such experiences, and he has provided a "behind the scenes" look at one. Available online is the eighteen-minute video called "John Mayer 'In Repair': One Song, One Day," which covers a twelve-hour period during which

CREATIVITY IN MUSIC

he joins with a guitarist-bassist and drummer to create a new song for an album.[10] They go from nothing to a polished recording. The video illustrates a number of processes that account for a successful session of group creativity:

- The participants have musicianship that is strong and flexible. They have experience to draw from, and they know a lot of the same things. They know the same conventions of music (for example, that same kind of chords and progressions, rhythmic expectations, etc.). And of course they have good musical ears. They can play by ear and improvise, which allows them to musically interact well together.
- As they work together, they are establishing social roles in the group process. While one person may be a designated leader (like John Mayer in the suggested video), that person should still be accepting of the others' ideas and input. Especially in an artistic venture, all members of a group must feel that their contributions are important and valued by the others.
- Participants must effectively communicate with each other. They can do so in a variety of ways. As with any group, they can talk together. When it comes to sharing creative ideas, this is not always easy. Sometimes an idea is so good that it is immediately and unanimously embraced. But other times, group members must find tactful ways of voting down ideas. Also, good musicians communicate nonverbally during performance. They use eye contact, facial expression, and physical gestures. Especially interesting is how the most advanced performers actually communicate with each other *through the music they play*. For example, during a rock band's jam session, the bass player may use his chosen bassline to signal to the others in the group where the chord progression should go. Or the drummer may signal through a drum fill how he thinks the tempo or rhythmic activity should change.
- Even in a group session, creativity requires reflection. All the musicians in a productive group know the value in experimenting musically and discovering what their spontaneous performance produces. But they also recognize the need to periodically step away from their instruments and microphones, and with fresh ears evaluate what they've created. Psychologist Howard Gardner

has suggested that exceptionally creative individuals are willing to risk failure in order to experiment freely, and spend much time reflecting on and refining their work.

Yes, it is impressive what a few great musical minds can come up with together!

MAKING MUSIC LEARNING MORE CREATIVE

An overriding purpose of this chapter has been to assert that just as all people are capable of creative thinking, all musicians can engage in musical creativity. Nobody should avoid creative musicianship by dismissing the idea with "I'm not really a creative type." Being creative is not a type or a personality trait, it is a skill. And like any skill, being musically creative is developed through experience, and it can possibly be "fast-tracked" through deliberate practice.

Young musicians need not aspire to be composers or songwriters to reap the benefits of greater creativity in their music studies. At least once in their lives, all musical people should have the experience of writing a song, that is, creating original music to personally express their inner feelings or their real self. The song-creation process can be a personally enriching and cathartic experience whether the produced work is ever performed for anyone or not. With the newly gained insight of a songwriting experience, young people will likely approach all their music activities differently. In addition, with an upgraded creative musicianship, young musicians can bring a deeper perspective to the professionally composed music they perform.

If trying to compose an entire song seems unmanageable (or perhaps a song seems inapplicable to an instrumentalist), young musicians can still gain much by simply composing an original melody for their primary performance instrument. And it must be said that the composing is *not* about writing things down in music notation. With young musicians who may not be confident in their notation skills, it might be best to speak of "making up" new music rather than "writing" music. Composing is really about the generation of original music. Preserving that creation can be done using music notation, but it can also be done in an audio recording, or simply by "writing it" into one's memory. This is also where improvisation and composition can intersect. When musicians spontaneously make up a melody or musical riff—that's improvisation—if they then decide its good enough to "keep" and work further with, once they've "saved" it somehow, it now becomes composition.

Students who are reluctant to dive right into improvising and composing can still dip their toe in the waters of creativity by performing a familiar piece in a musical style they know it is not "supposed" to be done in. Or they can experiment with performing a known melody with a wide variety of contrasting emotional characters.

Musical creativity can take many forms. This chapter now closes with ideas for teachers, parents, and peers to encourage young musicians to increase the creativity in their developing musicianship.

Make Music in Nonjudgmental Contexts and "Brainstorming" Sessions

Whether in an art studio setting or in a meeting room in the corporate world, there are well-accepted rules of brainstorming. There is to be no criticizing of ideas generated. Wild ideas are welcomed. In brainstorming, the goal is to strive for quantity over quality. The evaluation of ideas for "quality control" will be accomplished in another session.

Young musicians need to have some experience music making in a setting like this. Whether they do it alone in isolated practice or in a group setting, at times musicians should just turn off the critical voice within them. They obviously cannot take this approach with all their practicing and music-learning experiences, but in moments when they want to develop their creative musicianship, they need to adopt a mindset of exploring music, allowing for and even *embracing* the fact that making mistakes will occur.

By way of explanation, creativity consists of two equally important *but separate* processes. First is the generation of new material without primary concern about whether it is good or not. The second is subsequently judging the produced material with the purpose of revising and refining it. To develop music students' creativity, these two separate processes should be assigned as two separate exercises. In the initial nonjudgmental idea-generation phase, teachers and parent can support their young musicians by reminding them that producing bad ideas are just as valuable as the good ones.

Do Informal Practicing and Rehearsing

As is recommended at other points in this book, music-learning experience can be enhanced by drawing from the practices of vernacular musicianship. In an informal music-making setting, many young musicians can more readily find a "safe-mode" for experimentation. Aspiring vernacular musicians—those in rock, R&B, and jazz—are known for constantly "noodling," "fiddling," or "messing around" during their practice and rehearsal sessions in order to modify familiar music material and come up with entirely new stuff. When music teachers want to encourage student experimentation in their lessons, they need to be sure to step away from their position as authority who determines whether student work is correct or incorrect. Instead, they must let go of rigid plans and expectations and assume the role of facilitator, acting as a member in the community of learners, and being open-minded and responsive to students musical ideas.

Boost Creativity Through Collaboration

If young musicians have built positive relationships with musical peers, they may be more inclined to flex their creative muscles in a group situation. Whether paired up with one other person or in a larger group, some of the ideas offered above can be more easily implement in a collaborative setting. Some young musicians may do better with initial brainstorming, while others may be more immediately adept at the subsequent process of modifying and refining what's been produced. Put these two types of musicians together and creative synergy and productivity can follow.

Draw Inspiration from Others' Innovations

Instead of only idolizing performers for their virtuosic performance "chops" and great success in the music business, students can gain much from discovering past instances of musical innovation. They can read up on or watch online videos about famous musicians who were known for being especially creative. As they learn, young musicians may begin to take on the creativity-infused value systems of inspirational artists.

NOTES

1. Howard Gardner, *Creativity and Leadership: Making the Mind Extraordinary* (Los Angeles: Into the Classroom Media, 1988), video.

2. David Blum, *Quintet: Five Journeys toward Musical Fulfillment* (Ithaca, NY: Cornell University Press, 1999), 6–7.

3. WNYC Studios, "Help!" *Radiolab*, podcast audio, March 7, 2011. https://www.wnycstudios.org/story/117165-help. The quote from Elizabeth Gilbert begins at approximately 29:30 into the podcast.

4. Julia Cameron, *The Right to Write: An Invitation and Initiation into the Writing Life* (New York: Penguin Putnam, 1998), 10–11.

5. WNYC Studios, "Help!" The quote from Oliver Sacks begins at approximately 26:58 into the podcast.

6. Author W. Timothy Gallway has written a number of books applying his "Inner Game" approach. The first was: *The Inner Game of Tennis* (New York: Random House, 1974). He also collaborated with musician Barry Green on *The Inner Game of Music* (New York: Doubleday, 1986).

7. Anne Lamott, *Bird by Bird: Some Instructions on Writing and Life* (New York: Anchor Books, 1995), 93, 32.

8. Steven Pressfield, *The War of Art* (New York: Black Irish Entertainment LLC, 2012).

9. WNYC Studios, "Help!" The quote from Elizabeth Gilbert begins at approximately 36:56 into the podcast.

10. John Mayer, "John Mayer 'In Repair': One Song, One Day," YouTube video, 18:42. https://www.youtube.com/watch?v=_eWrQzNJgC8.

5

IMPROVISATION OF MUSIC

Most all people are fluent improvisers. The most common way is speaking. Every day, ordinary people talk with family members, friends, coworkers, and even strangers. And every word is created without a script. The vast majority of the time, spoken words are not rehearsed, but they still effectively express thoughts and feelings. A spontaneous conversation is anything but mindless. It's probably in such improvised interactions that people's minds are most engaged—listening to others' words, reacting cognitively or emotionally to what they hear, and offering heartfelt opinions of their own.

Despite being accomplished improvisational talkers, many people fail to develop this aspect in their musicianship. When college music majors are asked what performance skill they wish they were better at, improvising is always among the most common responses.

Clearly, improvisation is central to being a real musician. It includes being able to learn on the spot when working with other musical people, and being able to fake your way through a song someone requested that you only sort of know.

This chapter on improvisation explores the following ideas:

- The improvisations that skilled musicians generate are far from accidental. Although their music is spontaneously made, it is preceded—if only by a split second—by the idea or intention to make it.

- Improvisation is a musical skill that is acquired like any other. This type of musicianship can be developed by anyone with the right musical exposure, opportunities, and experiences.
- Many adult musicians have done so little improvisation over the years that they don't know how to develop the skill for themselves and may have become resigned to possessing a musicianship in which improvising is completely absent. If they happen to be music teachers, they may be unlikely to provide the instruction and experiences that their students need to learn the skill of improvisation.

NOT AS SPONTANEOUS AS YOU MIGHT THINK

We all make a myriad of decisions each day of our lives, with many coming on the spur of the moment. What coat do you grab as you run out of the house in the morning? What route do you take for your drive to work today? Do you hit the brake or the gas pedal at this yellow traffic light? In this sense, people largely improvise their way through life. Some of the decisions made are pretty sophisticated, as people draw on their past experiences, accumulated knowledge, and perception of current conditions. And they do so incredibly quickly. Especially in the case of that yellow traffic light.

Improvised music may be one of the most sophisticated forms of human decision making. Great improvisers can create a melody that, only moments before, they didn't know they were going to produce. So in this sense, musical improvisation is undeniably spontaneous. Yet closer consideration reveals that improvisation is not entirely unplanned and without preparation.

The music that skilled improvisers make is preceded—if only by a split second—by the idea or intention to make it. Musicians don't accidentally play that beautiful melody that fits the moment perfectly. It may be unrehearsed, but it's not random. They are expressing themselves. It's amazing that they're able to generate a musical idea so instantaneously, and do it repeatedly, and so quickly as each idea in succession is but a fleeting thought.

How do musicians come up with ideas that sound good in the moment? The ability derives from much exposure to the style of music they're performing in. Musical improvising is necessarily preceded by much music listening. Although some great books about improvisation can offer insights and some great music teachers can suggest exercises, these are merely supplements to the requirement of doing lots and lots of listening.

Having ideas of what to do is only part of the process. How do musical ideas actually get realized, and so effortlessly at that? To explore this, consider experiences outside of music for a moment (interesting insights can be gained by applying musical concepts to other aspects of human experience, and vice versa!). The world of comedy offers a good example. In his book *Blink*, bestselling author Malcolm Gladwell spends several pages considering the workings of an improv comedy group. He describes a team of comedians who can bring an audience to tears of laughter with a skit presented so smoothly that you'd swear they rehearsed it for days. Yet he clearly explains how "improv isn't random or chaotic at all" but rather "an art form governed by a series of rules." Gladwell maintains that with this kind of group improvisation, the amazing spontaneity results from hours of practice. The members of the troop have never rehearsed the specific skit that plays out for the audience in that moment, but they've all done similar skits like it many times before. He articulates the principle: "How good people's decisions are under the fast-moving, high-stress conditions of rapid cognition is a function of training and rules and rehearsal."[1]

To become a fluent musical improviser, practice is essential. But the meaning of practice here is broader than many musicians understand. Improvising can be developed by formal practice or by more informal means. Formal practice might entail repeating scales, arpeggios, and other motifs, in order to build a repertoire of assimilated patterns that allows the flow of improvising. But practice for improvisation can also be informal, and done in more authentic musical contexts. Many young musicians develop improvising skills by simply jamming together, messing around while playing a vibe, and just "noodling" on their instruments constantly. There's also a kind of middle ground between formal and informal practicing, such as when aspiring jazz musicians learn other performers' improvised solos from recordings. (This is sometimes called transcribing a solo, although they don't necessarily write it down.) They apply a deliberateness to this exercise that resembles formal practice, but the material is definitely authentic music.

Although the specific contents of any single improvisation are created on the spot, that music does not happen without advanced preparation and planning. By the time skilled improvisers hit the stage, they've logged a great deal of that preparation (through listening and practice), such that the planning or "ideating" happens almost reflexively. Jazz great Charlie Parker is said to have offered this advice: "You've got to learn your instrument. Then, you practice, practice, practice. And then, when you finally get up there on the bandstand, forget all that and just wail."

ADDITION BY SUBTRACTION

This chapter began with the assertion that most people are fluent improvisors. They do it constantly in speaking. With the vast majority of the words uttered every day, people do not write, rehearse, and memorize them before speaking them to other people.

This speech analogy may in fact be very similar to the processes of musical improvisation. This idea has been around for a long time, and empirical evidence supporting it is beginning to accumulate too. Some of the best recent research has been done by Dr. Charles Limb, who is a hearing specialist, surgeon, and brain researcher. He's also a musician. If you're not inclined to read his research articles, perhaps you'll consider watching his TED Talk "Your Brain on Improv."[2] In this talk, Dr. Limb eloquently shares his exploratory research with musicians who are skilled improvisers. The participants in his research carried out two different performance tasks: playing a memorized jazz solo and improvising an original one over the same chord changes. The kicker is that they do this in a functional MRI scanner, which captures images of activated areas of the brain.

Dr. Limb's results suggest that certain areas of the brain are much more active during improvisation than they are when playing music from memory. More specifically, the more active brain areas during improvisation are those thought to be autobiographical, including language centers for expressive communication. What's more—and this is really striking—some areas decrease in activity from memorized performance to improvisation. The area of the brain that essentially turns off is an area thought to be involved in self-monitoring.[3]

A good question is: how could *less* brain activity actually help in improvisation? Dr. Limb's theory is that what enables these improvisers' creativity is a "weird dissociation in the frontal lobe" of the brain. While self-expression needs to be boosted, *inhibition needs to be lessened*. In his words, "You're willing to make mistakes. You're not constantly shutting down all of these new generative impulses."[2] **AQ** In effect, what facilitates improvisation is more thought of one kind, but also much less thought of another kind. Incidentally, he also found similar brain activity in expert rappers engaged in improvised "freestyle" rapping, compared to when they recited an equivalent memorized rap.

These ideas are highly relevant to music making. First, in order to be a fluent improviser, musicians must develop the capacity to be spontaneously self-expressive. Back to the language analogy. Just as people can quickly choose and combine words to communicate their thoughts at any moment, musicians must possess a similar command of their musical instrument in order to be expressive on it. As in learning a language, this kind of fluency comes through much aural experience. A second important point is that performers must also be able to shut down the self-consciousness that can interfere with genuine expressiveness. This brings to mind the motivation concept of self-efficacy: to be truly competent with a particular skill, people must believe in their competence. In addition to developing the ability to improvise, musicians must also learn to trust in this growing musicianship. This can be an elusive goal, considering how so much music instruction is based entirely on error-detection (i.e., "let me tell you what's wrong with what you're doing").

Much can be gained by studying the processes of improvisation. Whether it comes by interviewing amazing musicians or by scanning their brains in action, the insights now available are extremely valuable. As Dr. Limb says in his TED Talk, "Artistic creativity is magical, but it's not magic."

RECLAIMING OUR NATURE

Improvisation—and creativity more generally—may be of special interest to those who missed these music-making experiences. Ask great improvisational performers how they do it, and they'll likely struggle to answer your question. They may not consider improvisation anything special. It's just what they do. It comes naturally. But for those who are not fluent improvisers, it really does seem like a special gift, and sadly, one they didn't receive.

But improvisation is a musical skill that is acquired like any other. Virtually all human beings are born with the capacity to be musical, and that includes through improvisation. Of course, that capacity becomes functional musicianship only with the right exposure, opportunities, and experiences. In these circumstances, young children develop musicality just as they develop language skills. As infants and toddlers, they hear people around them speak, and soon they imitate what they hear. If they hear people singing and making melodies, they reproduce those with their voices. Youngsters quickly build a huge vocabulary of words to express themselves. They similarly learn to match musical sounds to human feelings and gestures. Before reaching school age, children demonstrate relative mastery over their native language. They can recite memorized texts (e.g., "patty-cake patty-cake . . ."), narrate familiar stories with their own personalized spin, and spontaneously tell new stories straight from their imaginations. These abilities have direct musical analogs as well. Children can sing songs they've learned from people and recordings, make up personalized versions of familiar tunes, and create completely new songs right on the spot.

Perhaps the reason that music is often labeled a gift, while language is not, is that many people lose the musicality they developed in early childhood. This is not the case with language. Through middle childhood and into adolescence, most young people become more articulate and able to express themselves with words. In contrast, musicality often atrophies. Additionally, when introduced to a musical instrument, many young students are not afforded the time and experiences necessary to acquire the same aural fluency on the instrument that they've developed with language and that they began developing through singing.

So how do we develop improvisation skills in young musicians? Ideally, we let them continue doing what comes naturally. Young children are eager improvisers. School playgrounds are filled with spontaneous music. Hand a young kid a musical instrument and his or her impulse will be to experiment on it. This natural inclination underlies a call for free improvisation made by Northwestern University music-education professor Maud Hickey. In her 2009 article "Can Improvisation Be 'Taught'?" (published in the *International Journal of Music Education*) Dr. Hickey presents improvisation as a disposition that needs only be enabled and nurtured in young people. She rejects the typical ways that improvisation is done in school music classrooms (when it's done at all). For example, she challenges whether creativity is truly being fostered through a call-and-response activity, in which the quality of a student's improvised response is determined by how well it matches aspects of a teacher's call. Instead, Dr. Hickey endorses free improvisation, which is more rule-free and learner directed. It engages musicians in simultaneous sound exploration, which demands careful listening and reacting. She explains, "The sounds of a free improvisation session, if truly free, do not necessarily produce an 'aesthetically pleasing' product, and are certainly something an audience of parents may not understand, much less enjoy."[4] Not worrying about whether listeners will like it or not sounds to me like the lessening of inhibition that Dr. Limb's brain research supports.

Dr. Hickey admits that she's advancing a rather extreme position to provoke thought and dialogue. One need not whole-heartedly accept her approach in order to learn from it. The context for understanding her position is this: children are natural improvisers, but they can lose that disposition through underuse or neglect. The majority of high-school band and orchestra students lack even the most basic improvising ability on their primary instruments. And surely there are many adult musicians—including music teachers—who have done so little improvisation over the years that they don't know how to begin to learn the skill for themselves, let alone facilitate that learning for someone else.

ENCOURAGING IMPROVISATION IN MUSIC STUDENTS

As described above, speech and language learning ideas can be useful in music, including for offering practical suggestions to young musicians who need to reacquire a natural approach to improvisation. The following suggestions apply to both music students and the adults guiding their musical growth.

Listen to Music

It is essential that young musicians listen to music. They need to listen to a lot of music and listen to it frequently. They need to listen to the styles of music that they wish to improvise in, including recordings and live music when possible.

Listening to music as background while doing homework or chores around the house is fine, but young musicians also make time to listen carefully to music. With repeated listening to a recording, they should try humming along with the music as a way of testing just how familiar they are with it. At points when they cannot hum exactly what's on the recording, they should try to hum something that sounds good to them. And just like that, they're already improvising.

Play Music by Ear

Another important activity in developing improvisation is playing music by ear. Teachers can have kids try to reproduce songs that they know, whether they're pop songs, TV show themes, music from commercial ads, video game soundtracks, or Internet memes. Student instrumentalists can also build their ears by trying to play from memory music that they learned by notation, but haven't worked on for a while (not trying to visualize the notation of the music, but remembering the sound of the music itself). Kids have a lot of music aurally stored away in their minds, and they should be encouraged to use it. They will build their aural skills quickly if they regularly play by ear. And not just as a part of formal practice—teachers can tell students to keep their instrument handy whenever they're watching TV, playing video games, or on the Internet. When they hear music they know, they should try to play along.

Decrease Inhibitions

You can also support your young musicians' improvisation development by helping them identify conditions in which they can lower their inhibitions. This means finding the times and places in which they can explore music without worrying about whether they necessarily "sound good." Decreasing inhibitions may especially benefit young people who have grown up in home and schooling cultures that place a premium on doing things correctly and not making mistakes. There's a reason why people who insist that they're "nonsingers" still sing in the shower!

Spend Time Improvising Music

The final suggestion is to actually spend time improvising music. Yes, to get better at anything, you have to practice it. Encourage all musicians to improvise vocally and on their instrument. Many people need to start by shedding unhelpful preconceptions of what it means to improvise, such as, forget the image of the most advanced jazz performer firing off amazing riffs at lightning speed. Musicians with little experience improvising probably need to simplify, by just striving to create original *sounds* on their instrument, in some way that is expressive. (Don't think notes, licks, riffs, or melodies; just try to make expressive sounds.) Remind young musicians that improvisation should be a natural act, but it may not come naturally if they haven't done it in a while (since they were very small children). In that case, improvising will likely have to feel unnatural for a while before it starts to seem natural again.

These suggestions do not make up any specialized approach to improvisation. But they reflect that improvising can be a natural way to make music, rather than being a type of musical giftedness or a specialized skill reserved for jazz musicians or especially "creative types."

NOTES

1. Malcolm Gladwell, *Blink: The Power of Thinking without Thinking* (New York: Little, Brown, and Company, 2005).
2. Charles Limb, "Your Brain on Improv," TED Talk video. https://www.ted.com/talks/charles_limb_your_brain_on_improv.
3. Charles J. Limb and Allen R. Braun, "Neural Substrates of Spontaneous Musical Performance: An fMRI Study of Jazz Improvisation," *PLoS ONE* 3, no. 2 (2008): e1679.
4. Maud Hickey, "Can Improvisation Be 'Taught'?: A Call for Free Improvisation in Our Schools," *International Journal of Music Education* 27, no. 4 (2009): 285–99.

6

EXPRESSIVITY IN MUSIC

People's judgments of the *quality* of a musical performance is often based on the emotional expression they hear in the music. When hearing a recording, listeners want the music to *affect them*, to move their emotions, and enable them to feel something powerful. In a live performance, audience members want to be convinced that performers on stage are so personally involved in their own music making that the performance is primarily a natural sharing of strong of emotion between human beings.

Ideally, students approach music making with the goal of performing with heartfelt expression that will emotionally move their listeners. This, however, probably happens far too infrequently in rehearsal rooms and school auditoriums. Sometimes the only emotion student musicians bring to a performance is fear, as stage fright takes hold. What can teachers and parents do to encourage expressive musicianship and stave off the onset of anxiety in performance situations?

This chapter's coverage of musical expressivity is built around three main points:

- People's strong experiences with music are affected by the sound properties of performed music, but also very influential is what people bring to the experience as listeners or audience members.
- When taking in live musical performances, audience members rely heavily on visual cues, such as performer facial expression and bodily gesture, to perceive expressive communication.

- The three cognitive skills that underlie musicians' expressive performance are goal imaging, motor production, and self-monitoring. As performers develop these three skills, they improve the command and effectiveness of their expressivity.

EMOTION IN MUSIC: WHAT THE EAR HEARS

People have long wondered exactly *how* music can provoke strong emotions in listeners. It is amazing that merely hearing a certain sequence of sounds can cause people to have such intense feelings. And music can elicit a great *range* of feelings, depending on the way sounds are produced, how they are combined with each other, and in what order they're put. People's fascination with the expressive power of music can be seen in the great popularity of books such as Daniel Levitin's *This is Your Brain on Music*[1] and David Byrne's *How Music Works*.[2] As intriguing as this topic is for the general public, it is also of critical importance to musicians and music teachers.

Unless you believe in a sixth sense such as clairvoyance or telepathy, then you must accept that anything communicated from one person to another must happen via the senses of human perception. This is the case with musical communication. In order for the expressive sounds of a soloist to emotionally affect us, we have to hear it. (Of course, music can also be tactilely felt; and live performances can be seen . . . more on that below.) Sound has certain qualities that human ears can perceive. Once it happens, then the mind tries to make sense of the sounds, to find meaning in them. When, say, a cellist plays a sad melody and a listener responds by feeling a pang of regret, the sounds produced by the cello must have contained some very real acoustic properties that the ears and mind could handle.

Musicians who perform someone else's music begin their expressive communication process with some things already in place. One might say *a lot* in place. Whether it is classical musicians rehearsing from a composer's written score or a rock "tribute band" doing a cover version of their namesake's recording, they essentially start with the notes given to them. The pitches and rhythms—and the larger sequence/structure of the notes—are prescribed. Even so, the performers still have great expressive license here, in the elements of tempo, loudness/dynamics, and articulation. Additionally, some instruments are able to make changes in timbre, and add vibrato (i.e., slight wavering of pitch). These elements of sound are the "stuff" of music. It is what performers have to work with as they are trying to make their music emotionally affect listeners. And really, the elements identified in these last few sentences are a fairly comprehensive list.

Some musicians object to such a reductionist approach. They may fear that identifying the physical processes of music somehow ruins its "magic." This fear is unwarranted. The more people try to get "under the covers" of musical expressivity, the more they tend to be amazed by it! A better understanding of musical expression does not mean that it can be easily simulated through some formula of acoustic variables. And there is no reason to favor an educational approach that eliminates emotional language in favor of systematic attention to properties such as timing and loudness. But acknowledging the acoustic realities of music performance means this: A musician's expressive intentions will not emotionally affect listeners unless those intentions somehow become perceivable sound properties (again, barring any visual cues of a live performance). Audience members do not have direct access to the soul of a musician. They must rely on the outward expressions. And those expressions travel via sound wave to listeners' ears.

Past research on musicians' expressivity has shown one thing for certain: there is no singular way to do it. Some musicians prefer to visualize emotional images or scenarios. Others stick to the sound properties; they may mentally rehearse a version of their music with prominent expressive features, then try to realize that mental model in their performing. Still others attempt to muster up felt emotions in themselves, perhaps by recalling joyful or painful events from their lives.

All of these approaches can be effective. And all of them can fail. In fact, a musician's emotional intentions can actually interfere with the ability to perform expressively. This is particularly interesting. Sometimes musicians' expressive goals or expectations are so strong that they seem to bleed over into how they hear their own performances. In other words, they believe they are being expressive, but that belief is more based on their intent to be expressive, rather than an accurate judgment of the sounds they are producing.

MUSIC MADE FOR PEAK PERCEPTION

Clearly, music possesses the power to evoke human emotions, some of which can be extremely intense and meaningful in the contexts of people's lives. For many, live performance can do this especially well. Even in the current age of omnipresent digital recordings, live music is still in great demand. For those who take the stage as performers, it can be difficult to think of a concert solely from the perspective of a spectator. Performers are used to focusing on how best to produce expression and transmit feeling through their music. They may not think as much about how audience members receive expressive messages and how they experience emotion during performances. But the emotional rewards felt by concertgoers can be just as powerful—if not more so—than those felt by the people on stage.

These magical moments that are so cherished by musicians and music lovers have also been the target of psychologists' study for some time. The notion of *peak experiences*, first advanced by psychologist Abraham Maslow in the 1960s and 1970s, refers to mental states in which people have strong feelings of wonder, enthrallment, and ecstasy.[3] The 1980s and 1990s saw the popularization of the idea of *flow*, which describes how people can become so completely immersed in an engaging activity that time flies by and they feel the intrinsic rewards of the experience, free of self-consciousness.[4] One of the conditions of the flow state is a balance between the challenge of a task and one's skill in carrying it out. With this in mind, it is no wonder that music performance has been a frequent context for the study of peak experiences and flow.

Many musicians aspire to have peak performances in their activities. Ideally the presence of a public audience is not seen as a source of anxiety, but as an opportunity to further enhance the strong emotional rewards of performance. As musicians seek such experiences for themselves, most would also like to provide peak experiences for their audiences. Although music listening and concert attendance are not typically thought of as challenging activities or tasks, they can still be engaging and immersive and engender flow experiences. They are, however, clearly different from the act of performing music. Musicians can gain much with a better appreciation for all the factors that are present during a performance, specifically from the perspective of an audience.

Research on "strong experiences with music" has tackled a few of the more fantastic examples of music-induced peak experiences, such as transcendental and religious experiences, trance states, and synesthesia (visions of colors and lights stimulated by musical sounds). The research has also identified some of the most important contributors to audience members' peak experiences during a live music performance.[5] These influencing factors, in the broadest terms, are: (1) *the music*, (2) *the audience member*, and (3) *the performance*. All three interact to create the added dimensions that make live music so unique and powerful—the thrill of real-time vocal and instrumental production, the visuals on stage and around the venue, and the social aspects involving performers and audience members.

As explained earlier in this chapter, *the music* refers to performers' sound properties that make music expressive, including timbre, rhythm, pitch, tempo, dynamics, and articulation. It could be said that the art and craft of musicianship consist of choosing the right order, combinations, and variations of these properties in order to communicate to a listening audience. Other interesting research has provided insight into how certain musical devices can even elicit physiological responses from listeners. For example, a study of classical music lovers was able to identify some pretty specific musical triggers among Westerners. Among them, shivers were linked to sudden harmony changes, and a racing heart to instances of rhythmic syncopation.[6]

It seems a worthwhile endeavor to develop mastery over one's instrument in order to allow expressive musical devices to be carried out with control and precision. But simply producing expressive features in the music does not mean that performers always do so effectively. Other research has shown that even among advanced musicians, expressive intentions do not necessarily translate into the sound properties of performance.[7] Some musicians trust that their own emotions will naturally infuse their music and elicit the same feelings from listeners. It does not always work. As part of developing expressive performance skills, musicians need to direct conscious attention to the acoustic sound properties that they are producing—and how their sounded music is perceived by listeners—instead of dwelling only on their inner intentions to be emotional.[8] For example, consider a pianist who wishes to communicate sadness and longing in a melody. Her strategy for making the melody expressive may be to muster up feelings of sadness and longing in herself while performing. If her emotional process is engrossing enough, it could divert her attention from accurately hearing whether her sounded music contains features that will be perceptible to listeners. In fact, her own felt emotion could wrongfully convince her of the expressiveness of her music. As far as the music is concerned, listeners have *no other* way to access the heart of the pianist but by the way she presses the keys on the instrument (and the sound it produces). Musicians who have difficulty accurately assessing their expressive effectiveness in "real time" should consider recording their performance during a practice session so they can later listen to it and more objectively appraise their expressive performance quality.

Clearly *the music* (sounds produced by performers) is an important contributor to strong experiences with live music, and performers should diligently work on the expressivity they produce on stage. That said, they must not ignore the other two contributors, *the audience member* and *the performance situation*. *The audience member* refers to what an individual brings to a live music performance, and *the performance situation* refers to any performance factor that affects the individual's experience during the moments of the performance, including the visual aspects of what is on stage. Many things can affect an audience member's disposition and extra-musical associations during a concert, some of which are clearly outside of the control of any performer. (This does not mean, however, that performers should ignore the factor of the audience member altogether, as will be addressed below.) Performance situation factors, however, are often chosen—or passively accepted—by performing musicians. Anything that affects how concert attendees receive the sounds and sights of the performance can be extremely influential. This is why much preconcert time is spent on sound checks to ensure the best acoustics given the physical layout of a venue. But the visual aspects of a performance are also critically important. Cellist Alisa Weilerstein has gained considerable notoriety in the classical music world because, aside from her impressive cello technique, she is very physically expressive in performance. When asked about it, she has pointed to the moving and dancing that rock musicians commonly do onstage, and said "it always struck me as sort of surprising that people would find that strange in classical music."[9]

Concertgoers take many cues about emotionality from what they see in musicians' facial expressions, bodily movements, and other physical attributes. Quite a few research studies have confirmed that what people hear—or *think* they hear—can be heavily influenced by what they see.[10] Even among musically sophisticated audience members, judgments of musical quality are often biased by such factors as performer attractiveness, wardrobe, and stage behavior. There is also the *prestige effect*, by which listeners' perception can be skewed by whether they believe they are hearing, say, the "naïve interpretation" of a student musician versus a "bold rendition" by innovative expert. An inverse prestige effect also explains the famous (among classical music followers, anyway) Joshua Bell subway experiment, in which the world-class violinist went ignored while playing virtuosic repertoire in a busy Washington, D.C. subway station.[11]

No doubt some musicians lament that elaborate costuming, scenery, and stage "antics" may be used to compensate for poor command of one's musical instrument (i.e., technique, including sounded expressiveness). Such visual elements are often referred to as extra-musical factors. Perhaps, however, they are better understood as *para-musical* (i.e., from the prefix *para*, meaning "side by side" or "closely related to") in that the visual is necessarily a real part of live performance. No music can be perceived and understood outside of some cultural and personal context. Music performance has always been about more than the pleasantness of the sounds produced. Audio-purists should take heart, though, to know that research affirms that the sounded music does matter. But it is also clear that performers cannot afford to ignore the para-musical factors that affect perception of expressivity.

One clear message musicians can take from this research is that audiences do not parse out various aspects of live performance. Many times, an intense emotional response to music is less about the music, and more about the person taking it in. Music-induced peak experiences can often be cathartic in nature, characterized by the feeling of releasing inner emotions that want to be expressed. In one research study, listeners described music as a trigger, an outlet, or a way to deal with things that are "bottled up" inside. The researcher concluded that in many instances, "music does not create or change emotion; rather it allows a person access to the experience of emotions that are somehow already 'on the agenda' for that person, but not fully apprehended or dealt with."[12]

DO YOU HEAR WHAT I HEAR?

In many ways, the label "self-taught musician" is a misnomer. Even those who learn from YouTube videos avail themselves of the musical models of others. Most people who become skilled musicians only do so with the involvement of other people such as teachers, mentors, and musical peers, who serve important functions of giving feedback. Whether in the formal contexts of school classes or private lessons, or in the informal settings of a friend's garage or basement, budding performers learn a lot about their musicianship from other people's evaluation and advice.

At some point in their development, young musicians become less dependent on the appraisals of others and engage more in self-evaluation. Accurately hearing one's own performance, however, is not always a straightforward process. In fact, self-awareness may not be a strong suit for some performers. The appraisal of musicians' performances is the specialty of those who work in the field of audio production and sound engineering. Some within that profession have come to believe that many musicians are poor judges of their own performance. There appears to be a psychological phenomenon by which performers mentally replace what is actually sounded with an idealized version from their "mind's ear."

In some contexts, musicians can be unaware of aspects of their own performance. Lack of awareness is not surprising given that many of the expressive features that musicians put in their performances are done fairly automatically, presumably the result of much musical enculturation and practice. In one research study, when advanced pianists were asked to play a "deadpan" version of a melody—one with no expressive variations in tempo or loudness—they were consistently unable to do it.[13] But what is more interesting are times when performers believe they have added certain expressive features in their music, when in fact they have not. It may be that their musical intentions interfere with their ability to accurately hear their performance.

This phenomenon can be better understood through a model of cognitive skills used in music performance. When people make music, three kinds of cognition are going on:

- *Goal imaging* is the ability to generate a clear idea of what the music should sound like. Because music deals with sound, this "image" is primarily aural, but it may also include some visual or conceptual aspects (e.g., focusing on a "high point" in a phrase). While nearly everyone holds goal images of music in memory—it is how people can decide whether a particular rendition of a familiar song sounds good or bad—skilled musicians create precise images to guide their own performance.
- *Motor production* is the ability to carry out the physical movements and responses needed to sing or play a particular instrument. At first thought, this ability might not seem cognitive in nature, but remember that "muscle memory" resides not in the muscles but in the memory (i.e., the mind). Learning a physical skill involves remembering the "feel" of it. New motor skills require much conscious effort, but with adequate repetition, they can become automatic.
- *Self-monitoring* is the ability to accurately hear one's own performance. This is not always easy to do, which is why musicians can be surprised when they hear recordings of themselves ("Did I really sound like that?"). The importance of self-monitoring is seen in the research showing that musicians' motor learning is significantly impaired when they cannot hear their performance.[14]

It is the interaction between these three cognitive skills that accounts for improvement made in musicians' practice sessions. With a clear idea in mind of what they're trying to sound like (goal image), musicians can compare it to how they do sound (self-monitoring). Identifying discrepancies between the two should guide them in adjusting their technique (motor production).

Especially when performing unfamiliar music, carrying out these cognitive skills can demand all of a musician's attention. It may, in fact, demand more. Performers can cognitively "max out" just from concentrating on what they're trying to sound like and on executing the physical skills required. They may not have attentional resources available to accurately hear the results of their efforts.[15] This is why younger musicians can be so dependent on the feedback of others to know whether they performed something well. They simply cannot encode into memory both the goal and the outcome of performance. More experienced musicians may become so focused on the expressive intentions of their performances that they forget—or simply do not want to be bothered—to listen objectively to the sounds they're producing. Instead of comparing the products of goal imaging and self-monitoring to guide their performance, they linger over the goal.

This cognitive model can be useful to musicians as they attempt to diagnose their performance problems. It can also be useful to teachers—perhaps even music producers—when they are trying to get performers to change something about their playing or singing. The key comes in pinpointing where a breakdown is happening. Does the musician not have a good idea of what he or she is supposed to sound like? If so, goal imaging can be built through additional listening, both to recordings and expert models. (Certainly, school band directors would have an easier time in rehearsals if their students actually listened to band music.) Alternatively, some musicians' practice sessions may be ineffective because they are unaware of what they truly sound like. Perhaps they are practicing music that so challenges them technically that all their cognitive resources are devoted to merely producing the desired sounds on an instrument. In this case, it can be helpful to audio record their practicing and listen carefully upon playback.

Proposing the above three-component model is not to suggest that making music should be experienced as an analytical process. Although these cognitive skills underlie performance, musicians only try to bring them to the surface *while practicing*. Successful performance is marked by more fluid or "natural" music making. Through initial consciousness and careful repetition of practice, these cognitive skills become automatized in expert musicians. They likely become able to use extra-musical ideas—emotions, mental imagery, expressive metaphors—to more efficiently encode into memory the sounds and "feel" of performance that they acquire through experience.

LOOK YOUR BEST, SOUND YOUR BEST?

Every February, two media-heavy events bring a lot of attention to the expressive splendor of music performance. Touted as "Music's Biggest Night," the Grammy Awards are televised usually within a week or two of the musical-visual spectacle that is the Super Bowl halftime show.

Considering the musicians who headline these events, it would be easy to conclude that today's audiences believe that the best music is offered by the best-looking people. Or perhaps they just prefer to open their ears to those who are also "easy on the eyes." Of course, this is not just a modern phenomenon, nor is it limited to popular styles of music. The classical world has long featured performers who take the stage adorned in elegant gowns or suits, their appearance further ornamented by makeup, jewelry, and other accessories. Beauty, it seems, is a staple in most all kinds of music performance.

Research has established that what people hear in music—or perhaps more accurately, what they think they hear—is affected by what they see. Musicians (and producers) realize this and choose visual aspects of performance accordingly. Every December, Christmas music arrives with wintry images for the secular songs and religious ones for the sacred. New Year's Eve performances are put on amid eye-catching party scenes. As for the performers themselves, facial expressions, bodily movements, and other visible attributes can heavily influence audience perception of musical quality. This includes the performer's physical attractiveness.

It is no secret that physical beauty can make people think and behave differently than they normally would. TV news programs seem to routinely run hidden video social experiments on how beautiful women affect the behavior of men. Typically, two people act as motorists stranded on the side of the road; one is an attractive woman and the other is, well, not. The cameras capture just how quickly men stop to help the beautiful damsel in distress. Of course, visual bias has not always worked in women's favor, as veteran symphony musicians can attest. Female musicians were largely excluded from orchestras until behind-the-screen auditions were commonly instituted.[16] Sexism notwithstanding, beauty bias seems to extend beyond our highways and into our concert halls, and often serves to advantage musicians who have the right look.

There is research that suggests that listeners hear music as more appealing when it comes from a more attractive musician. In recent decades, an assortment of studies has shown that people tend to rate musical quality higher for performers who are judged to be physically attractive, as compared to those not judged as such.[17] And it is not just stage presence that is more highly appraised; the quality of their sounded music is rated higher. This effect has even been found among highly trained musical evaluators (graduate-level music study).

Simple physical beauty may have an effect, but there are other factors that influence how visually attractive a live performance will be. As already mentioned above, audiences are affected by the visuals cues of a performer's wardrobe, bodily gestures, and stage behavior. People perceive the sights and sounds of a music performance together. These two forms of sensory input interact with each other, and both are filtered by our preexisting tastes and beliefs (e.g., the prestige effect). These cause us to form expectations for performance, which surely vary according to our knowledge of the performance conventions of different styles of music. What is considered attractive in terms of wardrobe and bodily gesture can differ greatly from one musical subculture to the next.

With this in mind, physical attractiveness bias in performance is not merely a matter of a musician's absolute beauty (if such a thing exists). Rather, people form expectations of what a "good musician" looks like, and use them to judge whether particular performers look the part. This idea was highlighted in a music psychology research study smartly entitled "Posh Music Should Equal Posh Dress: An Investigation into the Concert Dress and Physical Appearance of Female Soloists." As the title suggests, people's opinions about the appropriateness of various performance attire—in this case jeans, a short nightclubbing dress, and a longer concert gown—were related to whether the performer played classical, jazz, or folk music. Judgments of appropriate dress coincided with higher ratings of musicality and technical performance ability.

The results of the "Posh" research reinforce the idea that judgments of musical ability are connected to physical appearance. The researcher made specific application of her findings to the performance practices of female classical musicians: "Women wishing to project a body-focused image should note that this may have a detrimental effect on perceptions of their musical ability."[18] This research underscores the fact that attractiveness is culturally defined, and certainly different musical subcultures define it differently. It brings to mind the controversies that can be stirred up when classical musicians stray from traditional concert dress. For example, the concerts of pianist Yuja Wang have often yielded reviews that spend just as much attention on her dresses as on her music making. And when critics have taken issue with her fashion sense, others have taken issue with that.[19]

Though some may disapprove of her wardrobe choices, fewer people would dispute that Yuja Wang is an attractive young woman. As mentioned above, a musician's physical attractiveness can contribute to favorable evaluations of her performing. But could it be that some people actually become better musicians because they are better-looking than others? There is some evidence to suggest this conclusion. Research has revealed some bias toward attractiveness *even when the performers were not seen*. In these cases, the performances rated highest in *audio-only* conditions tended to be those of more attractive musicians (as judged separately). In explaining this, researchers have theorized a deeper bias: as young musicians develop through training and other performance experiences, those who are more attractive garner more attention, opportunity, and encouragement. "It is conceivable," one researcher explained, "that the effects of attractiveness on progress in music may begin early in life, may be long lasting, and may be profound."[20]

Be it from a natural human mixing of sensory signals or the pervasiveness of beauty-driven media, there clearly exists an attractiveness bias in modern society. It should not be surprising that it is so evident in music. Though music may primarily be an aural phenomenon, it is well established that visual elements are quite consequential in the appraisal of musical quality. A meta-analysis of research on audio-visual music perception concluded that the visual dimension is "not a marginal phenomenon . . . but an important factor in the communication of meaning" and it "exists for classical as well as pop and rock music."[21] It seems that many of the top musicians of today understand this and stage their concerts accordingly. Perhaps with music, audiences should not judge a book by its cover, but research suggests it is an awfully hard habit to break.

MAKING MUSIC LEARNING MORE EXPRESSIVE

Expressivity really is *the thing* in music performance. As important as it is, though, many musicians fail to devote much instruction and practice time to it. Traditionally, formal music lessons tend to be dominated by technique instruction, and that, in turn, becomes the top priority that students take to their practice sessions. The thinking is that correct notes and rhythms are the most basic requirements to performing music well, and until those are in place, there is no point considering the "icing on the cake" that is expressivity. Perhaps the intention is to make expressivity part of the important work of "polishing" before a performance, but often the polishing work is cut short, and the real effect is downgrading expressivity to a low priority.

If given the choice, surely most audiences would prefer an emotionally moving performance with a few missed notes over a note-perfect performance that is devoid of convincing expressivity. In fact, there is no good reason for emotional expression to be anything but musicians' top priority in their preparing and giving a performance. This chapter closes with suggestions for better emphasizing expressivity in the music performance learning of young people.

Prioritize Expressive Performance over Technical Precision

When planning for an upcoming performance, instead of choosing music based on its ability to challenge and build the technique of student performers, try choosing music that will allow them to develop and showcase their musical expressivity. When technical aspects of music are considered most important, there exists the danger of choosing music that is too difficult for performers. In fact, many music teachers, and young musicians themselves, may prefer to choose music that is especially challenging technically, thinking it will force more practicing and result in greater skill development. Even when this strategy works, it is short-sighted: it signals to developing musicians that expressivity is a lower priority than technical accuracy, and it can reinforce performance as a difficult experience that is anything but feelingful, human, and emotionally fulfilling.

Performance is most rewarding—to performers and audience members alike—when the people on stage achieve (or approach) a flow-like peak experience state. For flow to be attained, there must be a balance of the challenge of the task with the musician's skill level. If the music is too difficult for performers, then they are more likely to feel anxiety rather than the optimal state in which confident expressive communication can occur. Rising to a seemingly impossible challenge is the stuff of Hollywood blockbuster movies and bestselling fiction, but it can be a harmful impediment to young musicians' expressive development.

Combine Approaches to Expressive Performance

In a young musician's performance learning, addressing musical expressivity can take several different approaches. Some music teachers and performers prefer to talk about expression in concrete terms, addressing the sound properties that make music expressive, including variations in loudness, tempo, and articulation. Others prefer a verbal approach that uses of imagery and metaphor (e.g., "sing like someone who's lost the love of his life" or "make the melody swoop and glide like a soaring eagle"). Still others opt for a nonverbal approach of aural modeling, in which student musicians try to imitate the expressive performance of teachers or expert musicians (via recordings).

All of these approaches can lead to improved expressivity in developing musicians' performance. Younger musicians especially can benefit from combining these approaches. Music teachers would do well, for example, to present a student with an expressive aural model ("Listen to how I sing this") *along with* an imagery-based description ("The melody should float like a leaf in the breeze") *and* direction about the sound properties ("I'm making the notes smooth and connected"). With this combined approach, students can learn musical terminology—both concrete and imagery-based—and better understand how to apply it to the sound properties of their own performance.

Record Performance for Later Self-Appraisal

It is good for musicians to record their performing, in order to step outside of themselves. The standard apps on today's smartphones and tablets offer the audio- and video-recording technology needed to capture an expressive performance in a practice session. Accurately evaluating one's own performance can be difficult for musicians to do during performance. Performing sometimes takes all of musicians' focus and energy, so that they do not have any attention left over to accurately monitor in real time how expressive they are. This can be easily remedied by making a recording to be used later for self-evaluation. This allows performers to take in the performance like an audience member, and judge the expressivity as an observer.

Dedicate Instructional Time and Practice Time to Expressivity

All musicians should consider expressivity a top priority. Teachers who want their student performers to be more expressive must devote lesson time to it and find effective instructional strategies to make expressivity valued and meaningful among students. If through the instruction they receive, student musicians become convinced of the importance of expressive performance, they are more likely to dedicate practice time to its improvement. Expressive performance is like any other skill: it is best improved through thoughtful and intentional practice.

Acknowledge the Importance of Visual Cues in Live Performance

Instruction and practice time devoted to expressivity should also include attention to the visual aspects of performance. One reason why people love live music is that the audience can take in visual expressive cues in addition to the sound qualities. In a live performance, facial expression, bodily gesture, and other visual aspects on stage are all extremely communicative, sometimes even more so than musical sound. In fact, in many settings, the visual aspects of a performance can be much more consequential to audience members. Those in attendance may be predisposed to hear the music more favorably if the visual aspects before them signal high-quality performance. Many young musicians who give recitals and concerts would benefit greatly by devoting more attention improving the expressive visual aspects of their performing. They may need to actually practice the facial expressions and bodily gestures they want to use in performance to communicate emotion to their audiences.

Take Audience Members' Perspective

Many highly successful performers make a special effort to know the types of people who are in attendance at their concerts. They not only practice the notes that they will produce on stage, but they consider the other factors that will affect the audience's perception. Instead of merely accepting the conventions of their performance genre—for better or worse—they more actively select the physical and social factors that hold sway in live music. They may even have some insight into the kinds of emotions their audience members seek to have stirred up or released by the music they take in.

Sometime the term "crowd-pleaser" is used pejoratively, as if performers doing what their audience enjoys is somehow a trait of artistic weakness. Perhaps there are times when this is true, but more often it is wise to show respect for the audience by recognizing its members as real "players" in a live performance experience. If providing an emotionally moving experience for those people is an important goal to performers, then they must acknowledge that an expressively successful performance depends on what audience members themselves bring to the experience and situational factors around the performance. Playing or singing for a crowd of engaged and emotionally responsive people will likely make the experience all the more rewarding for the performers themselves.

NOTES

1. Daniel J. Levitin, *This is Your Brain on Music: The Science of a Human Obsession* (New York: Plume/Penguin, 2007).
2. David Byrne, *How Music Works* (San Francisco: McSweeney's, 2012).
3. Abraham Maslow, *Toward a Psychology of Being* (New York: Van Nostrand Reinhold, 1968).
4. Mihalyi Csikszentmihalyi, *Flow: The Psychology of Optimal Experience* (New York: Harper Perennial Modern Classics, 2008).
5. Alf Gabrielsson, "Strong Experiences with Music," in *Handbook of Music and Emotion: Theory, Research, Applications*, edited by Patrik N. Juslin and John Sloboda, 547–74 (Oxford: Oxford University Press, 2011) and Alexandra Lamont, "University Students' Strong Experiences of Music: Pleasure, Engagement, and Meaning," *Musicae Scientiae* 15 (2011): 229–49.
6. John A. Sloboda, "Music Structure and Emotional Response," *Psychology of Music* 19 (1991): 110–20.
7. Robert H. Woody, "The Relationship between Musicians' Expectations and Their Perception of Expressive Features in an Aural Model," *Research Studies in Music Education* 18 (2002): 54–62; and Robert H. Woody, "Explaining Expressive Performance: Component Cognitive Skills in an Aural Modeling Task," *Journal of Research in Music Education* 51, no. 1 (2003): 51–63.

8. Patrik N. Juslin and Petri Laukka, "Improving Emotional Communication in Music through Cognitive Feedback," *Musicae Scientiae* 4, no. 2 (2000): 151–83.

9. NPR, "A Cellist is Chosen and Challenged," *Music Interviews*, podcast audio, May 28, 2011. https://www.npr.org/2011/05/28/136717840/a-cellist-is-chosen-and-challenged. The quote from Alisa Weilerstein begins approximately seven minutes into the podcast.

10. Klaus-Ernst Behne and Clemens Wöllner, "Seeing or Hearing the Pianists? A Synopsis of an Early Audiovisual Perception Experiment and a Replication," *Musicae Scientiae* 15, no. 3 (2011): 324–42.

11. Gene Weingarten, "Pearls Before Breakfast: Can One of the Nation's Great Musicians Cut through the Fog of a D.C. Rush Hour? Let's Find Out," *The Washington Post Magazine*, April 8, 2007. http://www.washingtonpost.com/wp-dyn/content/article/2007/04/04/AR2007040401721.html.

12. John A. Sloboda, "Empirical Studies of Emotional Response to Music," in *Cognitive Bases of Musical Communication*, edited by Mari Riess Jones and Susan Holleran, 33–46 (Washington, D.C.: American Psychological Association, 1992), 35.

13. Woody, "Explaining Expressive Performance."

14. Rachel M. Brown and Caroline Palmer, "Auditory-Motor Learning Influences Auditory Memory for Music," *Memory and Cognition* 40 (2012): 567–78.

15. Peter E. Keller, "Attentional Resource Allocation in Musical Ensemble Performance," *Psychology of Music* 29 (2001), 20–38.

16. Claudia Goldin and Cecilia Rouse, "Orchestrating Impartiality: The Impact of 'Blind' Auditions on Female Musicians," *The American Economic Review* 90, no. 4 (2000): 715–41.

17. Adrian C. North and David J. Hargreaves, "The Effect of Physical Attractiveness on Responses to Pop Music Performers and their Music," *Empirical Studies of the Arts* 15, no. 1 (1997): 75–89; Charlene Ryan and Eugenia Costa-Giomi, "Attractiveness Bias in the Evaluation of Young Pianists' Performance," *Journal of Research in Music Education* 52, no. 2 (2004): 141–54; Charlene Ryan, Joel Wapnick, Nathalie Lacaille, and Alice-Ann Darrow, "The Effects of Various Physical Characteristics on High-Level Performers on Adjudicators' Performance Ratings," *Psychology of Music* 34, no. 4 (2006): 559–72; Joel Wapnick, Alice-Ann Darrow, Jolan Kovacs, and Lucinda Dalrymple, "Effects of Physical Attractiveness on Evaluation of Vocal Performance," *Journal of Research in Music Education* 45, no. 3 (1997): 470–79; Joel Wapnick, Jolan Kovacs-Mazza, and Alice-Ann Darrow, "Effects of Performer Attractiveness, Stage Behavior, and Dress on Violin Performance Evaluation," *Journal of Re-

search in Music Education 46, no. 4 (1998): 510–21; Joel Wapnick, Jolan Kovacs-Mazza, and Alice-Ann Darrow, "Effects of Performer Attractiveness, Stage Behavior, and Dress on Children's Piano Performances," *Journal of Research in Music Education* 48, no. 4 (2000): 323–36; and Joel Wapnick, Louise Campbell, Jeanne Siddell-Strebel, and Alice-Ann Darrow, "Effects of Non-Musical Attributes and Excerpt Duration on Ratings of High-Level Piano Performances," *Musicae Scientiae* 13, no. 1 (2009): 35–54.

18. Noola K. Griffiths, "'Posh Music Should Equal Posh Dress': An Investigation into the Concert Dress and Physical Appearance of Female Soloists," *Psychology of Music* 38, no. 2 (2010): 159–77.

19. A music critic's review of a Yuja Wang concert that focused more on her appearance than her musicianship: http://articles.latimes.com/2011/aug/20/entertainment/la-et-concert-dress-notebook-20110820; and another music critic's critique on that review: https://www.washingtonpost.com/lifestyle/style/2011/08/10/gIQAMvtOBJ_story.html?utm_term=.29dcbb63bf05.

20. Wapnick, Kovacs-Mazza, and Darrow, "Effects of Performer Attractiveness, Stage Behavior, and Dress on Children's Piano Performances," 519. See also Ryan et al., "The Effects of Various Physical Characteristics of High-Level Performers on Adjudicators' Performance Ratings"; Wapnick et al., "Effects of Non-Musical Attributes and Excerpt Duration on Ratings of High-Level Piano Performances"; Wapnick et al., "Effects of Physical Attractiveness on Evaluation of Vocal Performance"; and Wapnick, Kovacs-Mazza, and Darrow, "Effects of Performer Attractiveness, Stage Behavior, and Dress on Violin Performance Evaluation."

21. Friedrich Platz and Reinhard Kopiez, "When the Eye Listens: A Meta-Analysis of How Audio-Visual Presentation Enhances the Appreciation of Music Performance," *Music Perception* 30, no. 1 (2012): 71–83. The quote is found on p. 75.

7

PERFORMANCE OF MUSIC

Along with the teachers and parents of music students, researchers studying music psychology are extremely interested in understanding how young people become proficient performers. Some research psychologists have focused their efforts on *expert* musicians; the assumption is that studying those whose music learning has been very successful can identify *what works*.

Research on expertise has identified deliberate practice as the most important contributor to performance achievement.[1] This finding certainly affirms the emphasis that music education has traditionally placed on practice, and it is the reason why young musicians' practicing is addressed so prominently in chapter 3 on motivation.

As universally acknowledged as practice is, likely every musician would agree that practicing is not the same as performing. The processes of acquiring music performance skills can be quite different from executing those skills in front of a live audience. The subject of "stage fright" is another hot topic in performance psychology as well as the field of music education. Most young children, upon learning a new song or how to make sounds on a musical instrument, are eager to show their new accomplishment to family and friends (and anyone else who will listen). Usually, however, as these youngsters grow up, making music in front of other people becomes a nerve-wracking activity pushed on them by proud parents and teachers.

Performance anxiety need *not* be an accepted fact of musical life. Performing music can be an enjoyable experience of sharing for adults and young people, as it is for young children. This chapter offers insights toward this goal, including these broad points:

- Musicians' thinking can be a powerful resource toward making performance a fulfilling activity. The beliefs and attitudes about music that they affirm can largely determine what performance will mean to them.
- Being musically prepared—even overprepared—is not always enough to prevent performance anxiety.
- Blurring the line between practice and performance can help young people make performing a meaningful and enjoyable culminating event for their music learning efforts.

TAKING STOCK BEFORE TAKING THE STAGE

When great musicians are on stage, audiences are amazed by how naturally the music flows from them. They display great energy in what they are doing, but it seems to happen without much obvious exertion. The performers communicate through their music, and it moves the thoughts and emotions of those who watch and listen. It would seem that in the ideal performance situation, this process happens almost organically, naturally driven by the musicians' inner passion and free of contrivance and strain.

This ideal situation, unfortunately, may be quite rare in today's concert halls. Musicians can become so preoccupied with the work involved in giving a public performance that they lose sight of their expressive goals. They would love to take the stage with clear minds and more fully channel the emotion they wish to communicate. But this can be an elusive endeavor. To make matters worse, sometimes the only emotion a musician brings to a performance is fear, as stage fright takes hold.

Because of the ideas described above, some may come to believe that performance success depends on shutting off the intellect. It can be an appealing prospect: quit thinking and planning and analyzing, and just trust that a love for music will produce an expressive performance, right? Perhaps not. Research on the psychology of music suggests otherwise. Cognition may, in fact, be the most powerful resource toward fulfilling performances. It is thinking—specifically a musician's beliefs and attitudes—that guides motivation patterns in musical activities. It is mindful and deliberate practice that most efficiently builds performance skills. And there is great value in our mind's capacity for reflection, that is, our ability to monitor our musical behaviors and even change the way we think.

Here is one example of how beliefs and attitudes can affect the way musicians approach performance. Some psychologists who study motivation have suggested that there are two broad orientations that people can have when pursuing something like music: ego-involved and task-involved. Those with an ego-involved goal orientation are primarily concerned about how others judge them through their musicianship. Performances are opportunities to garner favorable recognition . . . or to lose it. Those with a task-involved goal orientation think primarily about the musical activity itself. Their thought processes center on producing a performance that measures up to a self-set standard.

In research on goal orientations, *belief in musical talent* has emerged as an important underlying factor. Those who think of musical talent as an inborn stable trait ("either you have it or you don't") appear to be more likely to take an ego-involved approach to performance. They tend to think about how they would compare to other musicians and be concerned about looking bad. This is in contrast to those who believe musical ability is acquired through effort and practice; these musicians appear to be more likely to embrace new challenges and to do so out of personal interest. Furthermore, task-oriented musicians tend to employ more varied and in-depth strategies in their practicing. [2]

Performers have much to gain by examining their motivations, perhaps even using the ego- and task-involved goal designations. Musicians driven by ego goals—without much task involvement—are more likely to experience negative feelings in their music making. Their orientation may actually hinder the effectiveness of their practicing and make them more susceptible to stage fright. When musicians go into performances primarily concerned about how others will judge their musicianship, instead of focusing on expressive aims, they can worry excessively about wrong notes. Performance is no longer an opportunity to enjoy, but an ordeal to endure.

Simply being aware of one's thought processes heading into performance can be beneficial. In a particularly insightful and practical research study, college music majors were asked to complete a "diary" before fifteen performances during a school year. For each entry, always done within an hour before performing, they described their thoughts and feelings heading into their performance. Over the course of the fifteen performances, there was a significant decrease in performance anxiety reported by the music students. And note, these musicians were not directed to use any particular strategy to combat stage fright; they simply acknowledged in writing what they were thinking and feeling. It seems that even some honest self-awareness can have a positive therapeutic effect.[3]

It is safe to conclude that avoidance of thinking does not facilitate gratifying performance experiences. More likely, the key is being able to direct thoughts to the right things. For years, psychologists have treated anxieties of many kinds through *cognitive restructuring*. In this approach, people struggling with anxiety learn to change their thinking, primarily through self-talk. This does *not* entail reciting undue praise to oneself in a shallow "power of positive thinking" way. Rather, self-talk is used to monitor and reshape thought patterns, in order to replace irrational negative thoughts with more *realistic* and *task-centered* ones. The approach has shown to be effective with musicians. In one study, performance psychologists provided three workshops in which musicians were guided in examining their thought processes related to performance anxiety. They identified their typical negative thinking, and learned how to replace dysfunctional "all or nothing" thought patterns with more constructive ones. Even with this relatively modest intervention—just three hour-long sessions offered over a three-week period—the musicians experienced a significant drop in perceived anxiety while performing, as well as a significant increase in the quality of their performances, as determined by independent musical judges.[4]

Ultimately musical performances are judged by how expressive they are. As described in the previous chapter, reliably giving "feelingful" performances is not done accidentally or instinctively. Performers cannot simply shut off their minds just prior to taking the stage. Perhaps for some of the greatest musicians, their skills are so practiced, so polished, and so deeply rooted that they can deliver a stirring performance with their thoughts wandering to others things. But most musicians are not there yet, and instead have to employ their minds as they prepare to present music to an audience. They must also maintain mental focus during performance. There can be some serious drawbacks to stepping on stage preoccupied with worry about the performance—what's riding on it, what could go wrong, and other potentially threatening aspects. A better alternative is to focus thoughts on the music making, and that in its plainest context. Fundamentally, music is about the sharing of expression with others, done because it is a meaningful, enriching, and essential part of being human.

WHEN PRACTICE, PRACTICE, PRACTICE ISN'T THE ANSWER

It is an all-too-common scenario: Young musicians stand backstage about to go on, and they can feel the adrenaline coursing through their bodies. They may feel pounding in the chest, shallow breathing, and a swarm of butterflies in the stomach. As they take the stage, they notice shaking hands. It is bad enough that they have to experience this extreme unpleasantness, but they also worry that it will ruin how their music sounds onstage.

For those who've struggled with it, performance anxiety can seem like a fact of life. They may accept it as an inevitable part of performing. And accordingly, they may come to believe that they'll never sound in concert as good as they did in rehearsal. Performance quality—how accurate or otherwise "good" the music sounds to an audience—is paramount. So dealing with anxiety means somehow compensating for the drop-off in quality that happens onstage. "If I play it 95 percent well in rehearsal, but only 80 percent in performance," one might think, "then if I can get it to 110 percent in rehearsal, I can expect 95 percent on stage. Right?"

From this perspective, many have advised young musicians that the key to successful performance is overpreparation: practice your music so much that even your worst rendition still sounds pretty good. Practice so you know it incredibly well, then practice it some more so that your body will deliver it onstage without thinking, without trying. Then, according to this view, you can have utmost confidence and no reason to worry going into a performance.

Without question, practice is a necessity for building musical skills. But it is not always the key to overcoming performance anxiety. In fact, if musicians can play or sing the music well in rehearsal, but not in the concert, then additional practice may be quite a poor strategy for managing stage fright. Instead of accepting and coping with a drop-off from practice to performance, musicians should seek to remove the factors that diminish onstage quality.

Psychologist Glenn Wilson has divided the sources of musical performance anxiety into three categories: the task, the situation, and the person. Many musicians and researchers have found this model useful for understanding performers' anxiety issues and selecting effective treatments.[5] *The task* is the source of anxiety when musicians believe they are physically incapable of playing or singing their music; in such cases, additional practice *is* a viable treatment. However, *the situation* is the more likely source of anxiety when worry is brought on by the conditions of a public performance. Situational factors include the presence or absence of coperformers, the makeup of the audience, and any consequences of performance (e.g., an audition or competition). *The person* as a source of anxiety refers to the influential role that musicians' own thinking plays. As mentioned earlier in this chapter, performers' own thought processes can be empowering or debilitating.

As prevalent as performance anxiety is, the value of diagnosing its common sources has not been recognized. More common are recommended cure-alls, ranging from the silly ("imagine your audience in their underwear") to the simplistic ("practice, practice, practice"). Also popular are reactive strategies for confronting anxiety. Breathing and muscle relaxation exercises have been found effective for many, and some turn to beta-blocking drugs. Such advice reflects the fatalist attitude mentioned above, in which musicians accept anxiety as fact and resign to battling symptoms without considering what is causing them.

A preventive approach starts with identifying the source. While practicing the music to be performed (the task) is undeniably important when approaching a concert, much research suggests the influence of the performance conditions (the situation) and what goes on inside the heads of musicians themselves (the person).

Identifying the source of one's performance anxiety can be of critical importance. In a study published in the journal *Psychology of Music*, three researchers in the United Kingdom compared perceived performance-anxiety experiences of several different types of musicians, including classical, jazz, and popular. Across all participants, solo performance elicited more anxiety than group performance. Additionally, classical musicians tended to report higher levels of anxiety. The researchers concluded that the traditionally formal context of classical performance may create additional pressure and increase anxiety levels.[6]

That higher anxiety is linked to solo performance (vs. group) and classical contexts (vs. more informal) has been reported in other previous research. These clearly represent situational factors. Greater mastery over one's music (the task) through practice does not address the intense "on the spot" feeling of a public solo performance, or additional pressure that may be brought on by formal concert settings. Instead, musicians can deal with situational stress through mental rehearsals, in which they try to remain calm while vividly imagining aspects of public performance. When situational anxiety is particularly debilitating, performers may follow a program of systematic desensitization. In this treatment approach, a musician carries out a series of performances, learning to control physiological arousal while gradually progressing from least anxiety-inducing to most anxiety-inducing conditions.

In another recent study, British conservatory students underwent a "mental skills" training program that addressed sources of anxiety within the categories of the person and the situation. Participants learned to manage anxiety through goal-setting, cognitive restructuring (changing thinking through self-talk), and vivid imagery in mental rehearsals. Compared to a control group, those who received the training experienced a significant increase in their self-efficacy (i.e., perceived competence) toward performing. The post-training comments of these musicians "revealed greater levels of self-awareness, confidence, facilitative views toward and heightened control over anxiety, and healthier perspectives toward music-making."[7]

Extensive practice may not be the key to attaining performance success once onstage. Moreover, excessive practice may not lead to enjoyment of the experience. Not only can stage fright harm the musical product being presented to an audience, it can prevent musicians from enjoying performance for themselves. Musicians may benefit more from focusing not on the quality of their music—which may just drive them to more practice—but on finding greater "in the moment" awareness and reward for themselves during performance. This approach may prompt them to think more carefully about the situational factors that affect their performance experience and to reexamine their thought processes during music making.

BLURRING THE LINES

Many music teachers are real appreciators of clarity. They often emphasize to students the importance of having clearly define goals and employing strategies to attain them. Their approach is to break down tasks into smaller pieces, stages, and responsibilities, a common method for teaching and learning. If a future performance is understood as the goal, then a plan can be developed to work toward a successful performance. Teachers provide instruction on how to perform effectively. Student musicians practice individually, then, in the case of a group performance venture, the ensemble rehearses behind closed doors in order to coordinate their music making. This activity leads up to the performance, which presents to an audience the results of their efforts and improved musicianship.

This method works. A coming public performance is an effective motivator to many musicians—in some cases, the only thing that gets them to practice! And obviously for any large-scale production, advanced planning, organization, and division of labor is a must. But is it possible for other musical benefits to come with *less* clarity? Yes, there can be some real advantages to blurring the lines between practicing, teaching, and performing.

What might this blurring looking like? First, consider what defines practice (including group practice, a.k.a. rehearsal). Practice is the process of musicians in learning mode. They feel free to work on skills they want to improve. They receive instruction from teachers and interact with other musicians. They're focused on music making, and why it is important to them. In contrast, performance can be seen as a finished product, and one that is presented for the evaluation of an audience. At that point, the spirit of growth and exploration can be suspended. Sometimes the specialness of performance comes with a certain pressure—at best a "one shining moment" experience, but at worst a "do or die" mentality.

With proper blurring, performance can remain a meaningful and culminating experience for young musicians without losing the learning orientation associated with practice. Guitarist Pat Metheny once touched on this in an interview in which he recounted growing up in Missouri. His music learning really took off when he started playing gigs in the Kansas City area. "That changed my life and gave me an incredible head start," he said, describing how he learned so much while performing, especially by observing a particular piano player he gigged with often. "Watching him play was probably the best instruction I could get." Metheny went on to share how these early performances were key in his development. They were a virtual testing ground for the musicianship that later made him great.

Metheny's description of these gigs sound like practice, teaching, and performance—all rolled into one! What allowed these experiences to be so multifunctional for him? And most importantly, can these factors be applied to traditional music teaching to reap the benefits? Here are some considerations in doing so:

- Performance as presentation versus sharing. A presentational performance style is defined by a distinct psychological boundary between musicians and audience members. Music students may benefit from a more relaxed setting, or even a participatory style with greater interaction between performers and audience. Many music teachers have had great success using "informances," in which they and their students explain the processes behind their music as they share it. They can even involve the audience members in making music along with them (blurring the line between performer and audience).
- The occasion as special versus customary. People who have been part of a great concert or musical productions have felt the buzz of a big performance. But it may not be ideal if the specialness mainly comes from the performance being rare and "fancy" (i.e., so different from practice). When young people see performance as a frequent and regular part of being musicians, then they may be able to expand benefits from the experiences. In other words, they may then have the necessary mental wherewithal during performance to observe and learn from co-performers, and to push their own skill development.
- The goal as being error-free versus expressive. Achieving this goal can be challenging, especially when the performance is of com-

posed music learned from notation. The development of technique is critical, since a certain facility on a musical instrument is required in order to be expressive on it. But too often, young musicians come to believe that the main goal of performance is simply to "not mess up." To convince students otherwise, teaches must first believe themselves! Perhaps there is an alternative to the common music teaching approach of waiting until all pitches and rhythms are learned before adding in expressive elements; however, both can be addressed concurrently while working on a piece of music. It may even be preferable to give expressive aspects higher priority than technical ones.

The three points discussed above mainly blur the line between practice and performance. There are other lines that could be blurred as well, to the additional benefit of developing musicians, including blurring the line between practice and teaching. There are music cultures in the world—Balinese gamelan, for one—in which individual practice is unheard of; instead, music learners develop exclusively in group settings under the supervision of experienced musicians. There could also be benefits in blurring the specialized roles of musicians, such as encouraging students to simultaneously develop as performers and composers And many recording artists have achieved great notoriety blurring the delineations between styles of music, like classical, jazz, and popular music. These "crossover" musicians and "fusion" makers may be great role models for all.

ENCOURAGING BETTER PERFORMING FROM MUSIC STUDENTS

The opening paragraphs of this chapter mentioned the eagerness with which young children typically want to show others what they can do musically. It is easy to imagine a toddler who, after learning a fun song in preschool one day, insists on singing it for his entire family at the dinner table that evening. Can performance be this enjoyable for older people involved in more-organized musical ventures? It can be if it is understood as a simply human sharing of musical expression with others. The following suggestions aim to help young musicians move toward experiencing performance more as a rewarding artistic enterprise and less as an anxiety-inducing ordeal. And there are roles for their teachers and parents to support this goal.

Take Ownership of Performance Elements

Musicians typically have some firm ideas of what performance should be like, as related to expected repertoire, the musicians' attire, the setup of the performance venue, and onstage etiquette. But the common practices for these elements are not written in stone anywhere; they are simply conventions. Research suggests that certain situational factors tend to elicit considerable anxiety in performers. Such conventions of performance should not be regarded as nonnegotiable. Musicians may find that they enjoy the experience more if they can actively choose for themselves the elements of their performance.

Similarly, music teachers would do well to not mandate performance elements for their students. Rather, young musicians will benefit from participating in making choices. As explained in chapter 3, a sense of freedom and autonomy is a huge contributor to intrinsic motivation, which is essentially the opposite of anxiety (and an important facilitator of learning). This type of decision making may go a long way toward students' growth as independent musicians. If others have always overseen their performances—doing the scheduling, dictating the conditions, making all the decisions—it's unlikely that they will ever come to feel ownership of performance.

When teachers give students more decision-making power, they learn faster and perform better. And when musicians take ownership of more aspects of their performing, performances can be a true reflection of them, and as such become more personal and fulfilling.

Make Performing a Regular Activity

It is almost cruelly ironic that musicians who suffer from performance anxiety will naturally want to perform less, but their path to overcoming this negative emotion ultimately involves performing *more*. Perhaps the worst mistake in dealing with stage fright is to avoid performance. However, this doesn't mean that anxiety sufferers should just force themselves to give high-pressure recitals in order to overcome anxiety, taking the attitude of "whatever doesn't kill you makes you stronger."

A better approach is to gradually overcome anxiety. To do so in a systematic way, young musicians can make a list of as many kinds of performance scenarios as they can think of, then rank order them from least anxiety-inducing to most anxiety-inducing. Below are some sample variables that could factor into the amount of anxiety felt about a performance, organized by categories of who, what, where, and how:

Who

- By yourself
- With co-performers
- For no audience
- For an audience of family
- For an audience of friends
- For strangers

What

- Classical music
- Popular music
- Background music
- Teacher-assigned music
- Self-selected music
- Well-known music performed before
- New music never performed yet

Where

- In a small room
- In one's home
- In a large rehearsal room at school
- On an auditorium stage

How

- Performed from music notation (practiced)
- Sight-read from music notation

- Improvised music
- Performed from memory (no notation)

Drawing from this list, a musician might decide, for example, that a low-anxiety performance setting would be to perform with a co-performer friend, for a small audience of only a family member, at home, performing a well-known piece of popular music, from notation that they have practiced before. After the musician has been able to successfully manage anxiety with that type of setting, he or she might change one variable from each category to make it slightly more challenging anxiety-wise. The musician will gradually work down the list, making sure to manage anxiety successfully at each step before moving on to a more challenging situation. Eventually, the musician can face with some confidence the prospect of carrying out what was originally a high anxiety-inducing scenario, such as performing: by oneself, for a large audience of strangers, on an auditorium stage, performing a teacher-assigned piece of classical music, from memory.

Performance should not just be something that musicians strive to endure. It can, realistically, be something they enjoy. If they reflect on their performance life and realize that they never really enjoy it, they owe it to themselves to make changes. Perhaps they need to start performing a different kind of music. Or perhaps they need to perform in different settings. Or perhaps they "reprogram" their minds to change the way they think about performance. Changing deep-seated thoughts and attitudes is no easy task, but it can be quite helpful to view performance at its most human level—as simply sharing music with people who want to hear it.

Address Causes of Performance Anxiety, Not Just Symptoms

Imagine a musician about to take the stage and all she can feel is her racing heart, trembling hands, and shallow breathing. Maybe she even feels nauseous and she has trouble focusing her vision. How could anyone in this condition perform in a way that is expressive? That is, expressive of anything other than absolute dread! It is no wonder that overcoming performance anxiety is often equated to simply eliminating these troublesome bodily sensations.

Unfortunately, attending only to the physiological symptoms of anxiety can be like putting a Band-Aid on a gaping knife wound. These symptoms are a natural part of the body's "fight or flight" response, which kicks in when a person perceives a threat. In the case of a real threat—say, the proverbial saber-toothed tiger—these physiological responses are good. They help a person to more effectively fight or take flight. For musicians whose symptoms are not debilitating, they may benefit from preperformance exercises like deep breathing and progressive muscle relaxation.

It is often more important, however, to identify why performing is viewed as a threat, or what aspects of it are most threatening. Identifying the source of anxiety (then addressing it) is usually key if performance is to become an activity in which musicians can *be their best*.

Don't Treat Practice as a Cure-All for Stage Fright

Sometimes the performance task itself—playing or singing music—is in fact the source of anxiety. Additional practice is the solution when musicians find themselves taking the stage thinking, "I just don't know if I can actually perform this music. I've hardly ever done it before." For many performers, though, this is not the problem. They know that they can play or sing the music well, but they worry that they will not be able to do it once on stage. In cases like this, it will not likely help to simply prepare and overprepare the music through practice. Sometimes seeing practice as a cure-all for stage fright is really a resignation to anxiety, almost like saying, "If I'm overprepared, then when anxiety inevitably hits, the drop-off in my focus and control will still yield a decent performance." If playing/singing is not the problem, but doing so for an audience is, then more time in practice is not the answer.

This mistake is all too commonplace—and potentially destructive—in the musical world. In fact, many well-intentioned music teachers may unwittingly compound students' anxiety by telling them that "performance anxiety is your body's way of telling you that you need to practice more." So although it is the punchline to the old joke of how you get to Carnegie Hall, "practice, practice, practice" is *not* always the solution to overcoming stage fright.

Pursue Realistic Thinking

The term "catastrophizing" describes when a musician entertains fears of a horrible performance outcome. Catastrophizing is like a dark, agitating, ominous cloud out on the horizon. These negative thoughts are usually vague and exaggerated. Instead of realistically considering "what's the worst that could happen?" the catastrophizing performer fixates on some nebulous feeling of disaster.

Often identifying the problem of catastrophizing is far easier than determining a good solution. Some people mistakenly think that the only way to combat a torrent of negative thoughts is to overdose on positive thinking. The main problem, however, is not that the thoughts are negative, but that they are *irrational*. So replacing absurdly negative thoughts with equally unfounded positive ones will not likely do the trick. Imagine a musician who struggles with catastrophizing is able to convince herself, "No, I'm not a terrible musician doomed to fail. I'm an amazing performer, and I will give the best recital ever with no mistakes at all!" This positive thought is superficial, not based on having addressed and changed the original distorted thinking. At the first sign of performance trouble, she may find her inflated hopes dashed and quickly plummet to new depths of negativity.

Rather than thinking in terms of negative and positive, musicians should seek to replace irrational thoughts with realistic ones based on evidence. Also, they should shift the focus from what the audience may think about a bad performance, to what they (the performers) need to do to carry out the music making successfully. Positive thinking can help, but only to the extent that it is rooted in reality.

NOTES

1. Andreas C. Lehmann, John A. Sloboda, and Robert H. Woody, "Chapter 4: Practice," *Psychology for Musicians: Understanding and Acquiring the Skills* (New York: Oxford University Press, 2007); Andreas C. Lehmann and K. Anders Ericsson, "Research on Expert Performance and Deliberate Practice: Implications for the Education Amateur Musicians and Music Students," *Psychomusicology* 16 (1997): 40–58; and Anders Ericsson and Robert Pool, *Peak: Secrets from the New Science of Expertise* (Boston: Houghton, Mifflin Harcourt, 2016).

2. Bret P. Smith, "Goal Orientation, Implicit Theory of Ability, and Collegiate Instrumental Music Practice," *Psychology of Music* 33, no. 1 (2005): 36–57.

3. Michael E. Sadler and Christopher J. Miller, "Performance Anxiety: A Longitudinal Study of the Roles of Personality and Experience in Musicians," *Social Psychological and Personality Science* 1, no. 3 (2010): 280–87.

4. Sophie L. Hoffman and Stephanie J. Hanrahan, "Mental Skills for Musicians: Managing Music Performance Anxiety and Enhancing Performance," *Sport, Exercise, and Performance Psychology* 1, no. 1 (2012): 17–28.

5. Gerald Klickstein, *The Musician's Way* (New York: Oxford University Press, 2009); Andreas C. Lehmann, John A. Sloboda, and Robert H. Woody, "Chapter 8: Managing Performance Anxiety," *Psychology for Musicians: Understanding and Acquiring the Skills* (New York: Oxford University Press, 2007); Glenn D. Wilson and David Roland, "Performance Anxiety," in *The Science and Psychology of Music Performance*, edited by Richard Parncutt and Gary E. McPherson, 47–61 (New York: Oxford University Press, 2002); Elizabeth Valentine, "The Fear of Performance," in *Musical Performance: A Guide to Understanding*, edited by John Rink, 168–82 (Cambridge: Cambridge University Press, 2002).

6. Ioulia Papageorgi, Andera Creech, and Graham Welch, "Perceived Performance Anxiety in Advanced Musicians Specializing in Different Performance Genres," *Psychology of Music* 41, no. 1 (2011): 18–41.

7. Terry Clark and Aaron Williamon, "Evaluation of Mental Skills Training Program for Musicians," *Journal of Applied Sport Psychology* 23, no. 3 (2011): 342–59. The quote is on p. 342.

8

THE HUMANNESS OF MUSIC

Music is an amazing human phenomenon. Virtually everyone likes music, and for many, it plays a huge role in their lives. Consider the fact that music—merely a sequence of sounds received by our ears—can actually elicit strong emotions that are otherwise reserved for real-life experiences! No wonder it is so captivating. The processes of making music are equally remarkable. Whether it is composing an original song, singing with heartfelt expression, or playing a musical instrument, many complex skills are involved. These activities require sensory perception, mental thought and planning, physical execution, and emotional sensitivity—and all at the same time. Yet, musicians further are able to coordinate their own efforts with others to create amazing musical products.

With the right conditions and experiences, people can become so musical that their performance seems effortless. This outcome contradicts society's general belief in innate talent; instead, music making is a skill that is acquired—not inherited—much like speaking and reading one's native language. Like language learning, human beings are hardwired for becoming musical.

One might say that to be human is to be musical. Consider the titles that other musical authors have chosen for their popular books:

- *You Are the Music: How Music Reveals What It Means to Be Human,* by Victoria Williamson, 2014.

- *This Is Your Brain on Music: The Science of a Human Obsession,* by Daniel J. Levitin, 2007.
- *The Music Instinct: How Music Works and Why We Can't Do without It.* By Philip Ball, 2012.

People have a predisposition for music, and music teachers have a long history of building on this capacity in young people, providing rewarding music-learning experiences, producing highly skilled performers, and generally being powerful, positive influences in the lives of their students. Yet some practices in music education seem to barely scratch the surface. Of the general population, relatively few students elect to participate in organized music activities as teenagers, and far fewer ever engage in any active music making as adults.

Music learning is best for kids when it is meaningful to them as human beings and representative of the realities in which they live. The coming pages of this final chapter explain and illustrate why *being musical* equates to *being human*. Readers can expect gain insight into these broad points:

- Music study is sometimes touted for its contributions to educational outcomes such as improved standardized test scores, or the development of self-discipline and leadership skills. Although skeptics easily challenge these so-called transfer effects, one thing is certain: music study is very effective in making young people *more musical*, which is a tremendously valuable outcome in itself, considering the importance of musicality to what it means to be human.
- In many real and meaningful ways, music is representative of the human condition, including in music's capacity to reflect the very best that human beings have to offer.
- Positive human relationships are critical in musical development, as they are in most aspects of life. Relationships between teachers, parents, and students can be extremely consequential in enabling young people to get the most out of their music-learning opportunities.

WHY BECOME MUSICAL?

Occasionally an article will appear in the media with a headline about the benefits of music to the human brain. For example, one might read online that practicing a musical instrument boosts motor and sensory brain development, that "uplifting music" boosts brain activity, and that even children who are "not musically inclined" can gain stronger brains with early music lessons.[1] Such media reports can find approval among musicians, music teachers, and arts advocates. Those who are personally convinced of the great power of music can feel a sense of affirmation from results of brain research.

Beyond the simple sensationalism of such brain-based claims—one neuroscientist warned against believing the "neuro-bunk" out there, saying that many media members and advertisers think they can better sell anything if they just "put a brain on it"[2] —there are implicit problems with claims that musical brains are better than other brains. For one, various types of musicians possess skills that can differ greatly. For instance, most formally trained musicians focus on technique development and performance from notation, whereas "never had a lesson" vernacular musicians often improvise and play by ear. Surely the brains of these two kinds of musicians develop very differently. More generally, findings of brain research are not easily communicated because the research itself is complex and detail oriented. Each study has limitations that must be considered when interpreting its results. Each one addresses only a small aspect of brain function, and contributes but a small piece to a large body of literature that is useful in answering bigger questions.

Such limitations can be lost when media writers share research in ways that a general readership will find interesting. Consider a *Journal of Neuroscience* study that scanned the brains of formally trained musicians—professionals and university-level music students—who began their training before the age of seven. Compared to later-trained musicians and nonmusicians, the early-trained musicians had greater white-matter plasticity in the corpus callosum. This important finding can be difficult to apply practically to adult musicians and to parents of youngsters in music lessons. One Internet report about this study failed to hit the mark with its opening line, "If you played the recorder in first grade, you should thank your parents and music teacher now." Obviously, the vast majority of children who played recorder in elementary school have *not* grown up to become professionals or music majors, and thus not recipients of the brain benefits identified in the research.[3]

Overlooking important research details can lead to some exaggerated claims about the benefits of music, such as the so-called "Mozart effect" of the 1990s. The original study found that college students did better on a spatial reasoning task after listening to a ten-minute Mozart piano piece, as compared to sitting in silence or hearing a relaxation tape.[4] This very specific result somehow morphed into a "music makes kids smarter" movement that was embraced by many in the field of music education. In a grand display of irony, one governor aspired to raise the intelligence of his state through a rather dimwitted initiative, proposing a law that a classical music recording be issued to the parents of every newborn baby.[5] Surely there is value in broadening people's exposure to music, but doing so in hopes of improving traits like general intelligence is dubious. The wave of excitement for the Mozart effect eventually receded, as other researchers were unable to replicate the result of study. Perhaps also, people saw the folly of using *music* to improve math knowledge, instead of, say, simply offering better math instruction. Other recent brain-based music claims been disputed. University of Toronto psychologist Glenn Schellenberger is an outspoken critic of efforts to present music lessons as intelligence boosters. While emphasizing the value of music education, he asserts that to desire it for any transfer effects beyond music "is a complete waste of time."[6]

A good starting point is to apply some common sense to claims that music affects other abilities. In other words, if music does improve a certain cognitive function, is there a reasonable explanation for it? For example, one study found that school-based instrumental music instruction improved the verbal memory skills of children. Verbal memory has to do with how well people commit to memory words that they hear. The music instruction in the study included singing, rhythmic clapping, and pitch-identification exercises—all activities that involve listening. In explaining their findings, the researchers point to similarities in the brain's auditory processing of speech and musical sounds.[7]

Most people do not seek to become musical in order to raise their IQ or improve their visual-spatial reasoning. People get involved with music for the musical benefits. Musicians and arts advocates are best served by promoting the artistic, creative, and expressive outcomes of music experience. Musician-neuroscientist Daniel Levitin, author of the bestseller *This Is Your Brain on Music* once offered this insight into the question of why people should seek to become musical:

> There are benefits to having a society where more people are engaged with the arts, so even if music instruction doesn't make you a better mathematician or a better athlete, even if it only gives you the enjoyment of music, I think that is a good end in and of itself.[8]

OH, THE HUMANITY

Some of the most valued qualities of humanness have to do with the capacity to be open-minded, compassionate, and accepting of others. Unfortunately, human beings also have the opposite capacity to be ethnocentric and exclusionary. Surely the human battle of good versus evil—and people's different perspectives on it—has produced many of the best and worst moments of human history.

This aspect of humanity often plays out in very interesting ways in the musical world. People sometimes crusade for their preferred music with the same fervor that party loyalists campaign for their preferred politicians. And much as it is with political party-liners, often endorsement of a favored style of music goes hand-in-hand with condemnation of the presumed opposition. And although the destructiveness of political tribalism is decried by many (including those who are active participants!), very few seem to identify the harm that can be done when music people—be they performers, teachers, or listening connoisseurs—disparage other musicians and styles in an effort promote their own.

It seems, for example, that some people believe that the long-term success of classical music depends on convincing enough of the general public that other genres of music are comparatively inferior. Also, some supporters of serious jazz music seem to believe it is okay to mock in social media the musicianship of "lightweight" pop performers. And musical ethnocentrism surely goes both ways; there are many people who dismiss classical music as boring or jazz as weird without ever making an effort to understand the cultures, values, and purposes of these styles.

Becoming more musically broadminded can serve to advance young people's musicianship, as well as their humanness. Musical exclusivists can easily condemn nonpreferred styles if they judge all music by a single set of standards. Comparing apples to oranges is a well-known no-no that, unfortunately, still remains quite common in music circles. "Quality" is defined differently across the diverse styles that make up Western music. Classical music tends to value precise performance of a notated score; compositions are largely judged by such qualities as harmonic and textural sophistication and extended structural development. Jazz places a premium on harmonic complexity and rhythmic variation, with improvisatory performance being an important hallmark. Popular music typically values creativity outside of harmonic complexity, instead relying on sound (timbre) combinations, rhythmic groove, and melodic memorability; live performances are expected to have a strong visual component, through facial/bodily expression, gesture and dance, and performer–audience interaction. Applying the values of one musical style to another can result in quick rejection as "bad music." Calling a pop song bad music because it uses only three chords is like calling a classical composition bad music because casual listeners cannot sing along to the melody after one hearing. Yes, the crisp texture of an apple makes for a really bad orange.

Perhaps it is human nature, when faced with the unfamiliar, to compare it to what is already known and comfortable. Highly accomplished jazz musician David Berkman, in his book *The Jazz Musician's Guide to Creative Practicing*, encourages his readers to suspend judgment:

> Try to listen to a piece of music and not decide whether or not you like it. That's difficult to do. For many people, deciding whether or not they like a piece of music is the first thing they think of when they hear a new piece. Often younger players have strong ideas about who they like and who they don't. I still have favorite players . . . but I am more appreciative of more players now than when I was younger. A lot more of them are just too good not to like, even if you don't want to sound like them yourself.[9]

Although it may be difficult, young musicians benefit when they strive to be pluralists, accepting and even applauding those whose music making is different from their own. While it may be unrealistic to think government politics will ever give way to a spirit of nonpartisan acceptance and inclusivity, there is hope for music. People are capable of enjoying a variety of musical styles, and they can all truly coexist in the context of an enlightened individual's record collection or digital music streaming service.

The above exhortation for people to rise above musical partisanship underscores music's capacity to not just represent the human condition, but to represent the best that human beings have to offer. There is a growing body of research that suggests that music making may be an effective means for people to grow in empathy for others.[10] It could even be a way to break down prejudice between disparate cultural groups.[11] Many musicians are convinced of this, claiming music as a "power to bring people together . . . and to communicate and begin to connect with each other" with its ability to "knock down barriers quicker than any UN meeting."[12]

Other research has identified two broad conditions in which people tend to gain greater empathy for others: similarity and nurturing. Drawing from the principle of *similarity*, if people come to gain some familiarity with the music of a culture different from their own (or simply start to *like* the music), then they are more likely to feel they have something in common with the cultural group that they once considered so foreign to them. As for *nurturing*, group music making (e.g., singing together in a choir) has long been recognized for facilitating people's emotional investment in one another. People frequently find a sense of camaraderie and a social support system in such musical experiences, and come to see themselves as contributors to others' care and well-being, and understand and share their feelings.[13]

BEYOND THE PERFORMANCE OF MUSIC TEACHING

Most music teachers are musicians first, and then only later do they add the training for and experiences of teaching. Thus some enter the teaching profession with a performer orientation still fresh in their minds. They may approach teaching as a performance art itself. These music teachers may take their upfront position, and view their students as their own instrument, much like an organist sitting at the grand instrument, ready to work all the keys, stops, and pedals. Now, however, instead of pressing the keys and going through the motions to produce expressive performance, the teacher must "push the buttons" of students and enthusiastically execute instructional strategies to produce demonstrable learning in students. In this way, it is understandable why some music educators see teaching as a technical and expressive type of performance. Ultimately, however, it is a mistake to approach teaching as a musician performing on an instrument. Merely delivering instruction, making the right gestures, showing emotion, and being an expert in the subject matter are not enough. Although these qualities are important—very important—they do not ensure the effectiveness in communication and leadership skills required of teachers. Perhaps many a musician-turned-teacher needs a reminder: even before they were performers, they were first human beings.

The job of a professional conductor is quite different from that of a school ensemble teacher. And the job of a performing musician is quite different from that of a teacher giving private music lessons. The students in school ensembles and private lessons are developing musicians in need of much guidance and instruction. Productive relationships between teachers and students can take various shapes but must include one quality that exists in all constructive *human relationships*: mutual respect. Student musicians will not make much progress if they view their teacher with any suspicion, apathy, or contempt. Learners' attitude and motivation greatly affect how they take in instruction and how readily they apply it to their own music making. If they believe that their teacher genuinely cares about their musical growth and the emotional reward they get from music, then they will be tuned in to the teacher's message.

Parents can contribute much to the nurturing of good human relationships within their kids' musical experiences. In selecting a first music teacher for young children, parents should look for someone who will create a learning environment that is friendly, enriching, and even fun. Research has shown that this "warmth dimension" in an initial teacher is common in the biographies of people who go on to become accomplished musicians. As their musical kids pass from childhood to adolescence, parents should value teachers who exhibit a "stretch dimension," that is, effectiveness in encouraging and compelling students to do the practice and other activities to gain more advanced learning. When young people have entered more committed involvement in music activities, parents should encourage their kids to build positive relationships with musical peers. Friendships with high-achieving music students can enhance a young person's own musical growth. Parents should, however, be aware of musical subcultures that are overly competitive. Some people believe that competition is always good because, win or lose, it makes all competitors better. This perspective may hold up well in upper-level organized sports and in cut-throat business practice, but it can be quite destructive in the lives of some young music learners.

MAKING MUSIC STUDY MORE HUMAN

Gone are the days when parents dropped their children off for school and other extracurricular activities with the attitude of letting the other adult teachers, coaches, and group leaders "take it from here." It is not just tiger moms and helicopter parents who want to be involved. It is all loving parents, and let's face it: most parents *do love* their kids and love seeing them succeed. And they *really love* bragging about their kids' successes. Most parents willingly give their time, money, and energy to make sure their children are successful and they have something to brag about.

Parents can expect their children's teacher to welcome and appreciate their involvement. Over recent years, virtually every corner of education—including music education—has seen increased awareness of the importance of parents and teachers working together to promote children's learning.

The title of this book, *Becoming a Real Musician*, reveals what is perhaps its most important takeaway message: People *become* musical, and they do so through the right music experiences as children, and with the right kind of support from the adults in their lives. Unfortunately, not all music educational experiences produce a lasting musicianship in kids. In order for them to enjoy the gift of music for a lifetime, their music learning experiences must be relevant, practical, connected to the real world. Music making should not be just a pastime of childhood. Given what they need to become *real musicians*, young people will take into adulthood the skills and values for a musically active life. Whether they pursue music as a profession or an avocation for leisure time, they, like people have done for millennia before them, can use music to form life-affirming relationships with others and celebrate their humanness. Music students are most likely to become real musicians and experience the humanness of music when their learning experiences embrace the following recommendations.

Connect Being Musical to Being Human

Most people occasionally take stock of their own humanity and purpose on earth. They feel compelled to step back from their everyday lives and wonder, "Just what am I trying to do here?" Moments like this can lead to prioritizing values. People may determine the things that are most important to them and inwardly commit to them. This kind of process can lead people to appreciate aspects of the "big picture."

One of those aspects is the natural connection between music and humanness. Losing sight of the big picture, performing musicians can become obsessed with right notes versus wrong notes. And parents can worry and nag their kids about practice time. If they lose perspective by focusing on the "little picture," they may forget the primary purpose and benefits of music making.

Music is primarily about the sharing of expression between people. Consider music's capacity to evoke emotions, stimulate people mentally and physically, and build personal relationships through communal music making. Simply listening to music can be a very emotional experience, and performing it oneself can be even more so. For many people, listening leads to the desire to perform it (even if it is just singing along to a recording). Perhaps the most rewarding form of musical involvement is making music that allows one to express the *real* self. In other words, one's humanness is communicated through the music. In order for people to express themselves, they have to look inward. They have to know themselves, or at least know how they feel. Then they look outward to consider how to express themselves to the people around them. In this process, music provides a captivating medium for people to learn about themselves and learn about others. And learn about how people connect. And learn about the world in which these connections occur.

Music is a lens for considering core dimensions of humanness: growth . . . the passing of time . . . bodily motion . . . power . . . motivation . . . identity . . . consonance . . . conflict . . . emotion . . .

creativity. Some of the musical connections with these things are amazing. For example, a team of researchers found that the rate of slowing that musicians use in a ritardando (a decrease in the tempo of performed music) is "strikingly similar" to the pattern of deceleration that runners naturally take in coming to a stop.[14] Jazz trumpeter Chet Baker is purported to have said "I don't believe that jazz will ever really die. It's a nice way to express yourself." The simplicity of this statement is beautiful. Music will always exist because by its nature, it enables people to express their humanness. Music is critically important, yes, even in comparison to school staples such as math and science. To say that music is not important is to say that human expression is not important. And that is a position not easily defended.

Make Music Study Better Reflective of Kids' Musical Worlds

Through the late twentieth century into the twenty-first, music education has existed as a quaint but firmly entrenched throwback of sorts. Private music lessons have almost exclusively focused on developing young musicians' performance skills in classical music. Similarly, school music teachers have functioned primarily as directors of large ensembles such as concert bands, concert choirs, with the occasional string orchestra or jazz band. These traditional models of music teaching have persisted despite constant changes in the outside musical world. Within the profession, some have called to make music education better reflect the variety of young people's musical worlds, but the voices of the few revolutionaries have been drowned out by the more vocal majority proclaiming the benefits of formal music study as was done the century before. Most parents have thought that good old-fashioned music teaching would work for their children just as it worked for them when they were kids, and worked for their parents too.

But the tide needs to turn. Today's modern world offer kids more choices of activities—both inside and outside of school—like no generation before them. They seek empowerment and engagement in their own learning and development. With numerous activities vying for their time, they want convincing that music study is worthwhile and meaningful. Today's young people practically demand value, relevance, and fulfillment, or else they will quickly "unsubscribe" from an activity.

Teachers of private music lessons can no longer teach only classical music from étude books and time-honored repertoire lists. School music teachers can no longer specialize only as concert band directors, choirmasters, or orchestra conductors. These traditional ways of music making need not be abandoned wholesale. But music teaching in the future will become more inclusive and considerate of the learners themselves. As this evolution of music education happens, parents will have a critical role assuring that meaningful communication between teachers and students guides the musical growth.

Involve Students in Decision Making

Especially with young musicians, communication can be ineffective if students come to believe that their job is merely to take orders. It may be counterintuitive, but many times the best way to communicate is not necessarily the most direct way. Music students are not voice-activated robots. As parents know, simply telling children to do something does not always result in their receiving the message, let alone retaining it beyond the initial instruction. A conductor's message may be more effectively received if musicians are involved in the decision making, and even in the voicing of instruction. For example, instead of simply telling the ensemble to perform a phrase more legato, a conductor could sing it in that style and ask students to identify what sounded different. In general, the basic verbal strategy of questioning can increase the ensemble's overall attentiveness, and make real the student musicians' contribution in the rehearsal process.

Respect the Human Diversity of Young Musicians

Motivating students through the challenges of musical growth is critical. Supportive teachers and parents will hold realistic expectations, including in terms of attention span and the difficulty of music tasks undertaken. It is good to push music students' ability level—that is how growth happens. Overchallenging them, however, can be counterproductive if it only serves to induce anxiety, for them and their teachers and parents!

In any group of ten musical kids, there will likely be ten different motivational patterns related to music and performance. Some music students, when faced with a difficult passage in a piece, will be sustained through rehearsal because of the simple enjoyment they feel when making music in any way. Others will need to be motivated with extrinsic rewards (e.g., conductor: "give me fifteen minutes of focused work and we'll use the last few minutes of class to watch a YouTube video of an amazing professional musician's live concert"). Still other students, driven by a strong need to achieve in their musicianship, will see the passage simply as formidable challenge to be conquered.

Ultimately, the adults in musical kids' lives must be responsive to their students, willing to adapt their approach accordingly. Of course, it is easier to think "I've got my way of doing things" and the kids should adapt. But that attitude reflects adults who consider their leadership position one of power and privilege, rather than support and responsibility. Effective leaders are able to change their modus operandi, even if it means reducing their own prominence. After all, it is not a teacher's instruction that yields musical improvement, but the learners' reception and application of it. The more adults' messages are effectively received (not just delivered), the more musical kids use opportunities to grow their musicianship, and in the process feel more empowered to lead enriching musical lives once they reach adulthood themselves.

NOTES

1. https://www.upi.com/Health_News/2013/03/17/Music-practice-helps-brain-development/64561363555666/; https://medicalxpress.com/news/2013-03-uplifting-music-boost-mental-capacity.html; and http://www.piedmontparent.com/PP/Making-Music-Builds-Brain-Power-in-Kids/.

2. Molly Crocket, "Beware Neuro-Bunk," TED Talk video. https://www.ted.com/talks/molly_crockett_beware_neuro_bunk.

3. The original research report is Christopher J. Steele, Jennifer A. Bailey, Robert J. Zatorre, and Virginia B. Penhune, "Early Musical Training and White-Matter Plasticity in the Corpus Callosum: Evidence for a Sensitive Period," *Journal of Neuroscience* 33, no. 3 (2013): 1282–90. The quote misapplying the research is from Makini Brice, "Early Music Education May Enhance Life-Long Brain Development," https://www.counselheal.com/articles/3845/20130212/early-music-education-enhance-life-long-brain.htm.

4. Frances H. Rauscher, Gordon L. Shaw, and Catherine N. Ky, "Music and Spatial Task Performance," *Nature* 365 (1993): 611.

5. History.com editors, "Georgia Governor Zell Miller Proposes Writing 'The Mozart Effect' into Law," This Day in History, January 13, 1998. https://www.history.com/this-day-in-history/georgia-governor-zell-miller-proposes-writing-the-mozart-effect-into-law.

6. Nick Collins, "Learning Instrument Does Not Make Children More Intelligent, Experts Claim," *Telegraph*, February 18, 2013. https://www.telegraph.co.uk/news/science/science-news/9876911/Learning-instrument-does-not-make-children-more-intelligent-experts-claim.html.

7. Ingo Roden, Gunter Kreutz, and Stephan Bongard, "Effects of a School-Based Instrumental Music Program on Verbal and Visual Memory in Primary School Children: A Longitudinal Study," *Frontiers in Psychology* 3 (2012): 572. doi: 10.3389/fpsyg.2012.00572.

8. Collins, "Learning Instrument Does Not Make Children More Intelligent, Experts Claim." The quote from Daniel Levitin is found at the end of the article.

9. David Berkman, *The Jazz Musician's Guide to Creative Practicing* (Petaluma, CA: Sher Music Company, 2007), 115–16.

10. Lynda Laird, "Empathy in the Classroom: Can Music Bring Us More in Tune with One Another?" *Music Educators Journal* 101, no. 4 (2015): 56–61.

11. Maria Do Rosário Sousa, Félix Neto, and Etienne Mullet, "Can Music Change Ethnic Attitudes Among Children?" *Psychology of Music* 33, no. 3 (2005): 304–16.

12. The quote of "power to bring people together . . ." is from jazz flutist Steve Jordan, and the quote "knock down barriers . . . " is from drummer Steve Jordan, both from Jenny Boyd, *Musicians in Tune: Seventy-five Contemporary Musicians Discuss the Creative Process* (New York: Fireside, 1992), 114, 116.

13. Betty A. Bailey and Jane W. Davidson, "Effects of Group Singing and Performance for Marginalized and Middle-Class Singers, *Psychology of Music* 33, no. 3 (2005): 269–303.

14. Anders Friberg and Johan Sundberg, "Does Music Performance Allude to Locomotion? A Model of Final *Ritardandi* Derived from Measurements of Stopping Runners," *Journal of the Acoustical Society of America* 105, no. 3 (1999): 1469–84. http://www.speech.kth.se/prod/publications/files/590.pdf.

INDEX

acoustics. *See* sound properties of music
adolescence, 8
adversity, 37, 38
advocacy of school music, xi, 27–29, 122
anthropology, xi, 17–18
acquired skill. *See* skill acquisition
architecture, 27
athletics, xi, 5, 9, 28, 30, 35, 39
atrophy of musicality, 73
attitudes. *See* beliefs and attitudes
attractiveness. *See* physical attractiveness
autonomy, 8, 33–34, 38, 41, 47, 49, 50n2, 59

Baker, Chet, 122
Ball, Philip, 114
Beethoven, Ludwig van, 12
beliefs and attitudes, 98, 98–99
Bell, Joshua, 82
Berkman, David, 118
beta-blockers, 102
brain, 70–71, 78, 114, 115–117
burnout. *See* quitting music
Byrne, David, 78

Cameron, Julia, 58
choice. *See* autonomy
classical music, 6, 17, 82, 102, 118, 124
cognitive skills of music performance, 78, 84–86
collaboration. *See* social collaboration.

comedy, 69
composing, 11, 53, 62, 106
concert attendance, 80, 82, 92–93
constructivism, 6
creativity, 11, 28, 30, 53–64, 71, 122

Deci, Edward, 43
decision-making, 30, 68, 107, 124. *See also* autonomy
defending music education. *See* advocacy of school music
development. *See* human development
drive to succeed, 35, 39
dropout. *See* quitting music
Dylan, Bob, 11

ear musicianship, 21, 26, 62, 74, 115
Einstein, Albert, 54
emotional
   expression, xi, 12, 28, 59, 63, 79, 81, 83, 84, 90, 92, 94n8, 98, 100, 105, 113, 122; life, 18, 22, 122; reward, 6, 29, 80; regulation, 18; response, 77, 78
empathy, 119, 120, 126n12
enculturation, xi, 25, 36, 40, 72, 74
enjoyment, xi, 103, 106, 124. *See also* intrinsic motivation
entertainment, xi, 1, 5, 19, 27–31
error detection. *See* self-monitoring
everyday experience, 18, 19, 23, 27, 29, 67

experimentation, 6, 25, 53, 54, 63, 64, 72, 104
exploration. *See* experimentation
expressivity, 2, 77–93, 105
extrinsic motivation, 33, 36, 39–40, 42–45, 47, 49, 124

failure, 42, 55–56, 61. *See also* adversity
feedback, 49, 55
feelings, 11, 39, 41, 99, 119, 122
fight or flight, 110
Fleming, Renée, 5
flow, 80, 90. *See also* peak experience
free improvisation, 33, 72
freedom. *See* autonomy
fun, 6. *See also* intrinsic motivation

Gallway, Timothy, 59, 65n6
Gamelan, 106
Gardner, Howard, 54–55, 56
genres of music, 17, 106, 117
giftedness, 21, 28, 38, 56, 71, 75, 99, 113
Gilbert, Elizabeth, 58
Gladwell, Malcolm, 69
goal imaging, 85, 91
goal-setting, 36, 45–46, 50, 99, 103, 104
Grammy Awards, 86
Green, Lucy, 25

Hickey, Maud, 72–73
high school. *See* adolescence
human development, 1, 2
humanness, 2, 4, 8, 10, 13, 17, 19, 22, 23, 80, 100, 113–125

identity, 8, 14n5, 18, 27, 30, 32–33, 122
imitation, 56, 57, 59
improvisation, 12, 67–75
independence, 23–24, 84, 107
informal music making, 22, 24–26, 46, 48, 69
informance, 105
inhibition. *See* self-consciousness
inspiration, 56, 58, 64
intelligence, 27
intrinsic motivation, 6, 11, 25, 29, 31, 33, 34, 35–36, 39–41, 46, 48, 80, 107
investigator of music, 46, 50

jazz, 6, 60, 70, 75, 102, 118, 122

karaoke, x

Lamott, Anne, 59
language. *See* speech
Latifah, Queen, 5
leadership, 20–21, 33–34, 114, 125
lessons, 1, 3, 6, 8, 21, 84, 89, 115, 123
Levitin, Daniel, 78, 114
Limb, Charles, 70, 71, 72
listening to music, 26, 61, 68, 74, 79, 80, 83, 86, 90
live performance, 12, 77, 80, 80–83, 88, 92, 92–93, 98, 101, 104, 106, 107–111
love, 1, 8, 31, 32, 34, 36–37, 37, 41, 42, 44, 121

Ma, Yo-Yo, 55–56
magic of music, 71, 79, 80
major in music, 31, 32–34, 67, 99, 115
marching band, 33–34
Mars, Bruno, 5
Mayer, John, 60–61
meaning (in music), 14n7, 47, 78, 114
memory, 85
mental rehearsal, 103
Merriam, Alan, xi
Metheney, Pat, 104–105
motivation, 11, 35–50, 97, 99, 104, 122, 124
motor production, 85
muscle memory. *See* motor production
Mozart, Wolfgang Amadeus, 55, 116, 126n5

National Anthem, 5
natural music making. *See* nature of music
nature of music, 10–11, 71, 75
Nebraska, 31, 33
nostalgia, 2, 24, 121
notation (of music), 12, 62, 78

O'Neill, Susan, 3

Parker, Charlie, 70
participatory performance, 18, 19, 30, 31, 105. *See also* informal music making
peak experience, 80–83

INDEX

peers, 20, 26, 41, 49, 57, 120
perfectionism, 53, 56, 59
performance anxiety, 13, 46, 59, 77, 97, 98, 99–103, 106, 107–111
personalization, 7, 47, 107
physical attractiveness, 82, 86–89, 95n19
physicality of music, xi, 32, 85. *See also* motor production
Picasso, Pablo, 54, 57
planning, 68, 70
playing by ear. *See* ear musicianship
politics, 117, 118
pop culture, 5
popular music, 6–7, 17, 32, 57, 82, 102, 118. *See also* vernacular musicianship
practicing: deliberate, 26, 62, 69–70, 86, 92, 97, 98; effectiveness of, 99, 106; informal, 26, 64; misuse of, 101, 102, 103, 110; motivation for, 22, 39, 42–46, 47, 48, 49–50, 104; solitary, 25, 41
presentational performance, 13, 18, 30, 105
Pressfield, Steven, 59
Presley, Elvis, 36–38
prestige, 82, 88

quitting music, 3, 20, 21, 22, 23, 36, 40, 42, 48, 114

rap music, 71
realness, x, 1–13, 113, 121, 122
recording, 61, 84, 91
Red Hot Chili Peppers, 5
rehearsal, 41, 104
rewards. *See* extrinsic motivation
role models, 56, 64
Ryan, Richard, 43

Sacks, Olivrer, 58
school music, 6–7, 8, 23
self-awareness. *See* self-monitoring
self-consciousness, 55, 58, 58–59, 63, 70–71, 72, 74, 80, 99
Self-Determination Theory, 43–44, 49
self-discipline, 11, 19, 25, 27, 41, 44, 59, 114
self-efficacy, 38, 49, 50, 71, 103
self-expression. *See* emotional expression

self-monitoring, 45–46, 61, 71, 84, 85, 91, 103
sensory perception, 78, 89
sexism, 87
social: bonding, 6–7, 8, 9, 18, 29–30, 33, 119, 120; collaboration, 6, 30, 36, 41, 60–62, 64; development, 32
settings, x, xi, 4, 13, 22, 38, 46
songwriting, 11, 32, 53, 58, 62. *See also* composing
sound properties of music, 77, 78–79, 81–82, 83, 84, 89, 91
Spalding, Esperanza, 44
specialness, 3, 8, 27, 105
speech, 7, 67, 70, 72, 73
spontaneity, 19, 67, 68–70, 71
sports. *See* athletics
stage fright. *See* performance anxiety
STEM, 19
Stravinsky, Igor, 54
strong emotions. *See* peak experience
success, 19, 23, 35, 42, 46
Super Bowl, xi, 5, 86
support of others, 1, 2, 10, 23, 37, 38, 43, 47, 49, 50, 119, 121, 124, 125
systematic desensitization, 103, 108–109

talent. *See* giftedness
taste, 117–118
teaching: as a mission, 2; effectiveness, 6, 10, 91, 92, 104, 114; learner-centeredness in, ix–x, 28, 30, 68, 73, 107, 119–120, 123
technique, 90, 105
TED Talks, 70, 71
teenagers. *See* adolescence
thought processes, 99–100, 101, 102, 103, 109, 111
threat, 47–48
transcribing music, 69
transfer effects of music study, 11, 20, 21, 27, 53, 114, 116–117
Turino, Thomas, 17–18, 18, 30

U2, xi

vernacular musicianship, 24–27, 40–41, 64. *See also* informal music making visual aspects of performance, 77, 81, 82–83, 86–89, 92, 95n19, 107

Waits, Tom, 58
Wang, Yuja, 88–89
Watts, André, 44
Weilerstein, Alisa, 82
Williamson, Victoria, 113
Wilson, Glenn, 102

Woolf, Virginia, 54
work ethic, 21, 33
world music, 17
writer's block, 57–58

YouTube, 22, 84, 124

zero history group, 60

ABOUT THE AUTHOR

Robert H. Woody is professor at the University of Nebraska–Lincoln, where he teaches courses in music education and music psychology. He is an author of *Psychology for Musicians: Understanding and Acquiring the Skills* and he has a blog about the processes of music making on the *Psychology Today* website.

www.ingramcontent.com/pod-product-compliance
Ingram Content Group UK Ltd.
Pitfield, Milton Keynes, MK11 3LW, UK
UKHW022124220326
469203UK00007B/41